HOLIDAYS AT HOME

Festive Decorating & Gift Projects

CREATIVE
HOME
ARTS
—CLUB—

Creative Home Arts Library™

HOLIDAYS AT HOME
Festive Decorating & Gift Projects

Printed in 2005.

Tom Carpenter
Creative Director

Julie Cisler
Book Design & Production

Heather Koshiol
Managing Editor

Phil Aarrestad
Principal Photographer

Bob Green
Assistant Photographer

Maggie Stopera
Susan Telleen
Stylists

Sue Banker
Jana Freiband
Zoe Graul
Nancy Maurer
Cheryl Natt
Cheryl Nelson
Contributing Writers

Special thanks to:
Terry Casey, Janice Cauley, Happi Olson, Nadine Trimble

1 2 3 4 5 6 / 10 09 08 07 06 05
ISBN 1-58159-241-8
© 2006 Creative Home Arts Club

Creative Home Arts Club
12301 Whitewater Drive
Minnetonka, Minnesota 55343
www.creativehomeartsclub.com

CONTENTS

INTRODUCTION

The Season's Star, page 94

4

The holidays are a magical time. The cool weather and long evenings at home invite you to get ready for the festive season ahead.

That's what *Holidays at Home* is all about: Helping you beautify your home, create gifts and prepare for December celebrations.

- Create warm *Seasonal Accents* with decorating projects to make every room look festive and happy.

- Build *Traditions* by creating meaningful holiday mementoes for your family.

- Make the season shine with craft and decorating projects from *Winter Wonderland*.

- Make *Gifts for Giving* with these thoughtful, easy-to-create gift ideas.

- Finish all your gifts (handmade or purchased) with unique *Gift Wrapping* ideas.

Seasons Greetings Fold-Out Card, page 126

- Set a *Festive Table* with great projects that will add spirit, joy and elegance to any event you host.

Full-color photographs display each project and guide you step-by-step. *Holidays at Home* will make preparing for the holidays as much fun as the holidays themselves. And remember—you don't have to wait for December to get started.

Pick a project and kick off your holiday season today!

Candy "Cracker" Place Cards, page 138

CREATIVE
HOME
ARTS
—CLUB—

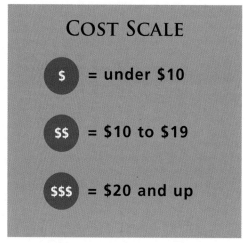

COST SCALE

$ = under $10

$$ = $10 to $19

$$$ = $20 and up

1
SEASONAL ACCENTS

Decorating for the holidays means transforming our spaces from "everyday" to "festive!" Here, you'll find ideas for **Seasonal Accents** that will help you add that special sparkle, whimsy, elegance (or all of the above) to your home.

SHIMMERING SNOWFLAKE MANTEL CLOTH

Trap snowflakes between sheer borders for an elegant look. Completing the project requires minimal sewing skills. Alternatively, you could fuse the project. The finished size is 48 inches long and 11 inches deep to fit a 48-inch-wide by 6-inch-deep mantel.

- ⅝ yard (60-inch-wide) solid white sheer fabric; 1 yard if mantel is wider than 48 inches
- ¼ yard (60-inch-wide) print sheer fabric; ½ yard if mantel is wider
- 23 (3-inch or less) foam snowflake shapes; more if mantel is wider
- Matching thread

TOOLS

- Shears
- See-through ruler
- Fabric marker
- Sewing machine or serger
- Iron
- Pins

$

1 From solid sheer fabric cut a 58- by 11½-inch rectangle and three 3½-inch wide strips (one 58 inches long and two 8½ inches long). From the print sheer fabric, cut a 9- by 52-inch rectangle. To form corner at end of long strip, pin short strip, as shown, and stitch, using a ¼-inch seam allowance, or serge. Repeat on other end. Press seams.

2 Place border strip and rectangle right sides together and stitch, using ¼-inch seam allowance, or serge. Turn right sides out, pushing corners out. Press edges. Measure and mark lines along border about every 3¼ inches to form "pockets" for snowflakes. If necessary, adjust lines to come out at corner. Stitch on marked lines, securing beginning and end of stitching. Place snowflakes and other small shapes in "pockets."

3 Press ½-inch fold around the one long and two short sides of sheer print rectangle. Place fabric, centered and right sides up, over the sheer lining fabric. Make sure there are no loose threads inside pockets. Pin in place, covering about ½ inch of border. Stitch along edge of fold. Press a ½-inch fold along two remaining raw edges. Pin together and stitch near fold.

HOLIDAY WALL POCKET

Make this fabric wall pocket to hold holiday cards or a small holiday floral arrangement (just insert a small piece of floral foam). Choose a panel print, overall print, brocade or velvet. A purse handle, purchased at a craft store, becomes the hanger. Beads can be added to the handle shown.

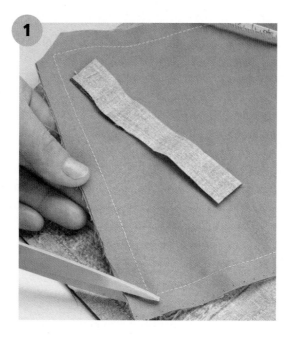

1 Cut fabric for front and back, 8 by 9 inches (or appropriately for panel print). From lining fabric, cut 2 pieces ¼ inch smaller on two sides and bottom than main pieces. Cut 1½- by 5-inch piece for tabs from either fabric. To sew "pouch," place pieces right sides together and use a ½-inch seam to sew around two sides and bottom. (Contrasting thread was used for photo.) Sew lining together in similar manner. Fold tab in half lengthwise, right sides together and sew, using ¼-inch seam. Turn and press. Trim bottom corners on "pouch" and lining.

2 Turn "pouch" right side out, pushing out corners. Fold ½ inch toward wrong side on "pouch" and lining, and press. Put lining into "pouch," aligning edges; pin at seams. Cut doily in half and sandwich in front, centered and between fabrics. Pin. Sew front section together, stitching close to folded edge.

3 Cut tab piece in half. Fold tabs around ends of handle. Sandwich tab between back fabrics and near seam. Pin. Repeat for other side. Sew section together, as above. If using handle where beads can be added, place beads on handle before sewing. If adding raffia, do so after the sewing is done, using large-eyed needle.

SNOWBALL WREATH

Celebrate the childlike wonders of winter with a playful snowman. This snowman won't melt, even if it's hung inside!

- ¼ yard white polar fleece
- Polyester fiberfill
- Baby stocking cap or winter hat
- 1 piece orange felt
- 7 (½-inch) black pompoms
- ⅛ yard colorful polar fleece
- ⅛ yard blue polar fleece
- 9-inch round styrofoam base
- 9 (2½-inch) styrofoam balls
- Package of artificial snow
- 2 small branches for snowman's arms
- Pipe cleaner

1 **Head**: From white polar fleece, cut two 9-inch circles. Sew circles together, leaving a 2-inch opening. Turn right side out, and fill it with polyester fiberfill. Sew closed and top with stocking cap. Sew hat edge to the back of snowman's head. To anchor hat on front, use a little hot glue underneath the hat.

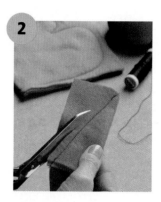

2 **Carrot nose:** Fold a 4- by 4-inch piece of orange felt in half. Sew a line diagonally from one corner of the felt to the opposite corner of fold, backstitching at both ends. Cut away excess felt, turn right side out and fill with fiberfill. Turn edges to inside and sew carrot onto snowman's face, with the seam facing down.

3 **Eyes and mouth:** Hot-glue 2 black pompoms in place for eyes and 5 black pompoms for the mouth.

4 **Scarf:** From colorful polar fleece, cut scarf approximately 36 inches long and 3 inches wide. Cut fringes on each 3-inch end. Hot-glue the scarf's center to the back of the snowman's head.

5 Hot-glue the snowman's head to the top center of the styrofoam base. Press it down for a minute or two until it has firmly adhered. (If the base cracks due to the heat, put a little hot glue in the crack and hold together until cooled.)

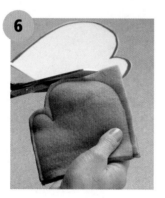

6 From a 4½-inch square of paper, make a pattern for wide mittens. Use pattern to cut 4 mitten pieces from blue polar fleece. Make two mittens by sewing two pieces together; turn right side out.

7 Poke a pencil into a styrofoam ball to hold it while you are working with hot glue. Drizzle hot glue over ball's surface and roll ball in artificial snow. Continue until ball is completely covered. Hot-glue all but two snowballs onto the base, holding each in place until glue cools.

8 Pull scarf ends through to front and tie it, hot gluing down any parts of the scarf as necessary. Insert one branch arm into each mitten and hot-glue in place. Hot-glue each mitten closed. Hot-glue a snowball to each mitten. Curl mitten around ball and hot-glue into place. Hold each surface down until glue has cooled. Hot-glue each branch into place onto back of base. For added strength, let hot glue cool completely, then squirt some hot glue onto the top of each branch and let cool completely. Twist pipe cleaner into a circle and hot-glue it onto the top back of the base as a hanger.

SNOWMAN STAR GARLAND

Turn a wooden star shape into a garland of snowmen to hang across your mantel, door or wall. Using easy painting techniques, anyone can create these snowmen, each with a unique personality. For a country-style garland, string snowmen together with twine or raffia.

MATERIALS

- 5-inch wooden star shapes with holes in 2 tips (as many as desired)
- Textured snow paint
- Masking tape
- Orange acrylic paint
- Black marking pen
- ¼-inch black pompoms
- Polar fleece or wool scrap
- 24 inches twine or raffia (for 1 single snowman)

TOOLS

- Ordinary dinner knife
- Toothpick
- Sponge
- Shears
- Glue gun and glue sticks
- Large-eyed needle (optional)

$

1 Cut thin piece of masking tape and tape top point of star where scarf and hat will be. (The points with holes are the "arms.") Spread textured paint on remaining area of star. Poke through "arm" holes with a toothpick. Using dry sponge, tap over the textured paint to even out the texture. Let dry according to manufacturer's directions, usually 2 to 6 hours.

2 When dry, remove masking tape. With marking pen, add black dots for eyes and smile. Slice a small sliver of a triangle off the sponge; dip in orange paint and add for carrot nose. Apply glue to snowman and add pompoms as buttons.

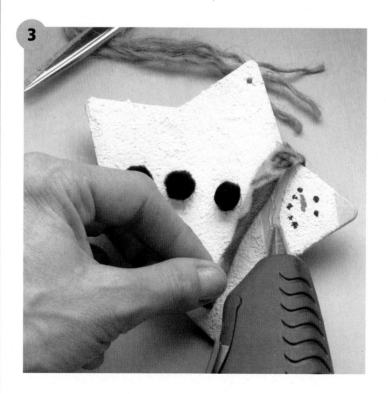

3 Cut each scarf ¼ inch wide and 6 inches long. Apply hot glue to back of "neck" and glue scarf in place. Cut triangular hat shape from fabric and glue onto "head." Cut twine into 12-inch pieces; thread through "arm" holes, using large-eyed needle if necessary. Secure with double knots. String snowmen stars together, as desired.

PAINTED HOLLY CANDLESTICK

Decorate a wooden candlestick with an "easy-to-paint" holiday design on the largest area. Purchase a new wooden candlestick at a craft store, or find an old one. Paint the candlestick with a primer first and then a holiday color.

MATERIALS

- Wooden candlestick
- Primer and spray paint
- Graphite tracing paper
- Holiday design such as holly or poinsettia - about 1 inch square
- Light green (fine tip) paint pen
- Red (medium tip) paint pen
- Medium green (medium tip) paint pen
- White (medium tip) paint pen
- Semigloss or gloss aerosol sealant

TOOLS

- Pencil and tissue paper

$

1 Prime candlestick, then paint base coat in a holiday color. Let dry. Trace design onto tissue paper. Place graphite paper under design with edges extending a bit beyond the tissue paper. Tape in place on the candlestick. Trace over design with a sharp pencil. Practice painting design on paper, if desired.

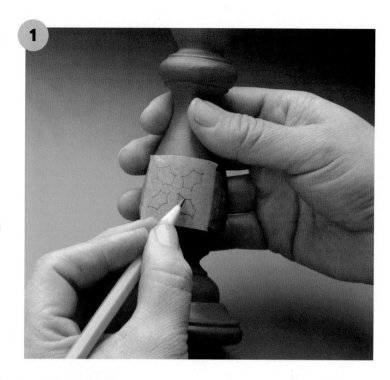

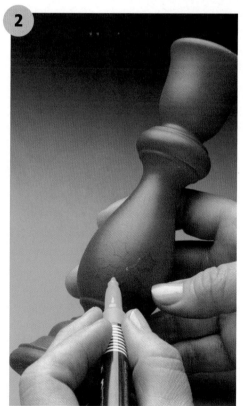

2 Outline and fill in each leaf with light green paint pen. Let dry. With medium green paint pen, paint over leaves again. Let dry.

3 With white paint pen, draw circles for berries in center of leaf design. Let dry. Paint over circles with red paint pen. Let dry. Add a small white dot for highlight on each berry, if desired. Let dry. Spray with aerosol sealant.

FAST AND EASY MANTEL COVER

Use polar fleece and bead trim to make this fast and attractive mantel cover. The finished size fits a mantel 48 inches long by 6 inches deep. Make it to fit any size mantel: Add 12 inches to the width and 6 inches to the depth of your mantel measurements.

1 Take mantel measurements. Measure, pin mark and cut fleece in rectangle 12 inches wider than mantel width and 6 inches deeper. The sample project measures 60 inches by 12 inches. Cut and remove 6- by 6-inch squares from "front" corners.

2 Starting at a corner, fold ribbon on trim, back on itself about 1/2 inch and pin to back of cover with ribbon just to the fabric edge. Using zipper foot, stitch from right side, about 1/4 inch from fabric edge. Just before end of stitching, fold ribbon back as before. Make sure to secure beginning and ending of stitching. While stitching, do not let polar fleece stretch.

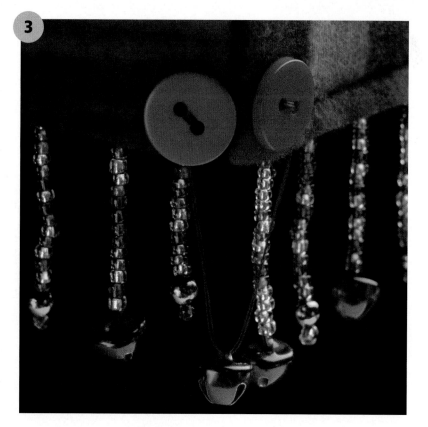

3 To hold corners together, stitch a button at "front corners." Form a loop with thread on each bell and, when cover is on mantel, place loop over buttons at corners.

MITTEN CHRISTMAS CARD GARLAND

Let these cute little pairs of mittens hold and display all your cheerful holiday greetings from family and friends.

1 **Mittens:** To create the basic mitten pattern, cut a piece of paper 2½ inches by 3½ inches. With the black magic marker, sketch a mitten as shown. Cut out the pattern. For the cuff pattern, cut a piece of paper 2½ inches by 1¼ inches. With the black magic marker, sketch the cuff; cut out pattern. From gray felt, use mitten pattern to outline 8 mitten shapes. Cut each shape with a sharp fabric scissors. From darker blue felt, use cuff pattern to outline 8 cuff shapes; cut out using fabric scissors.

2 To create smaller top mitten, use mitten pattern to trace 2 outlines on each of red, green and tan felts. With pinking shears, cut away approximately ¼ inch, so gray felt will show from underneath when colored felt is on top. (For the black felt, use chalk or just eyeball it; cut 2 smaller mittens with pinking shears.) Layer smaller pinking sheared mitten on top of the gray mitten and pin together. Using a running stitch, stitch the yellow embroidery floss around inside edges of smaller mitten.

3 To decorate the mittens, cut out 2 of each shape: star, heart, tree, holly/berry and apple. Stitch decorative shapes onto mitten tops. Do a second mitten with the same colors and pattern, turning everything over so that you end up with a right-handed and left-handed mitten.

4 Cut out a little rectangle of black felt and sew it to the middle of each of the darker blue cuffs. Stitch around the top of the blue cuff and stitch little snowflakes on both sides of the black felt. Hot-glue the cuff to the mitten top.

5 Cut a piece of gray felt approximately ½ inch by 9 inches to create a strip to connect the mittens, and to hang the mittens from the garland. Hot-glue each end to the back of the mittens to join 2 mittens into a pair.

6 Lay the completed mitten onto green felt and pin it down. With pinking shears, cut about ¼ inch overhang of green felt around the entire mitten. Hot-glue the completed mitten onto the green felt.

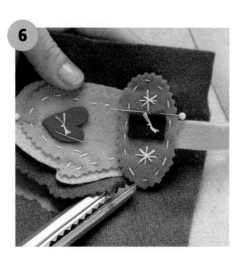

7 Hot-glue a clothespin onto the back center of each mitten, with the grasping part of the clothespin at the bottom of the mitten. Hang each mitten set from the garland, and add Christmas cards to them as you receive them.

HOLIDAY BOBÈCHE

Add some sparkle and holiday colors to a plain glass bobèche. For a decorative look, invert an embellished bobèche. Use it cup-shape-up to catch candle drippings.

1 From star garland, make a circle the size of bobèche's outside edge. Wrap about 3 lengths of garland into circle; hold in place by knotting with monofilament. With about 3 dots of glue to bobèche edge and garland, glue together, according to manufacturer's instructions. Hold in place with clothespins and allow to dry. (Some glues will take up to 24 hours to set.)

2 Tie end of bead garland with monofilament, then tie to star garland. **Tip:** Work with bobèche on candlestick with candle. Measure around bobèche's edge. Divide measurement into quarters and mark with pins. Measure and cut bead garland about twice as long as bobèche measurement. If you want bead garland to hang lower, increase this amount.

3 Divide garland into quarters and at the first quarter mark, tie Christmas ball loosely and hook both over the pin. Place the rest of garland and balls at each quarter mark. When satisfied with arrangement, tie where pin, garland and Christmas ball come together: thread monofilament under star garland and catch bead garland and ball. Remove pin and place dab of glue at intersections. Let dry. When completely dry, clip off any protruding monofilament. If desired, place some bead garland inside bobèche around base of candle.

CHRISTMAS TRAIN CENTERPIECE

Embellish a wooden toy train with a variety of holiday miniatures. If the cars on the train are hollow, drill holes from the bottom and add lights. Arrange it on a large tray to keep it together and for easier moving.

MATERIALS

- Wooden toy train (cars about 5 inches long and engine up to 6 inches long)
- Battery operated lights
- Miniature decorations for the sides of cars
- ½-inch brads
- Miniature garland
- Miniature Santa
- Miniature wrapped gifts or small items like musical instruments
- 12 feet soft-needle garland (for tray)
- Large tray, 20 by 14 inches (wood is best)
- Artificial snow (optional)

TOOLS

- Drill with ⅛- and ⅜-inch bits
- Wood glue
- Hammer
- Needle-nose pliers
- Glue gun and glue sticks
- Masking tape or duct tape

$$

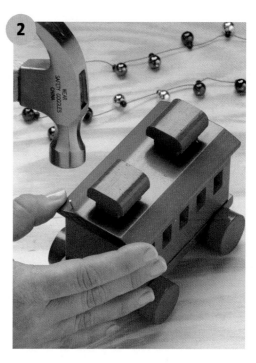

1 If wood train cars are hollow, drill holes for lights. First drill small pilot holes (with ⅛-inch bit), then drill each full-sized hole (with ⅜-inch bit). Drill two holes in larger cars and one in the caboose.

2 Determine placement of items along the sides, front of engine and back of caboose. Glue items to train with wood glue. (**Tip:** If train is painted with glossy paint, rough up the area where you will be gluing to make it hold better. This can be done by pounding small indentations with a brad.) Determine where garland will be hung and place small brads at the corners to hang them. Glue miniature presents and Santa into train engine and caboose.

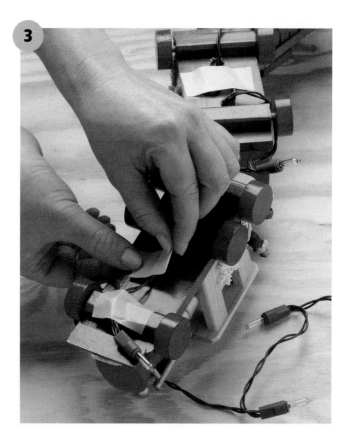

3 Arrange garland in tray. Determine placement of train. Add lights to train and tape wires to bottom to hold lights in place. Hide battery pack, place train on garland and add snow, if desired.

RETRO JOLLY OL' SAINT NICK

Retro crafts are back in style and this Santa fits the bill! Reader's Digest *magazines with a few simple embellishments are all you need to complete this craft.*

- 2 small magazines (*Reader's Digest* size)
- Clear tape
- Glue
- Red spray paint
- Red felt
- 19-gauge wire
- Santa doll head
- Cotton balls
- Cotton batting

TOOLS

- Scissors
- Wire cutter

$$

1 Fold every page of two magazines to a point by folding from each corner to the middle. Crease each fold and secure with tape.

2 Glue the two folded magazines together, cover to cover. Spray the glued books with red spray paint, using two coats of paint if necessary. This will become Santa's body.

3 **For arms:** Cut 2 pieces of felt 4 inches by 4½ inches. Cut 2 pieces of wire approximately 11 inches long. Cut 4 small pieces of red felt to look like mittens. Fold felt for arms in half at the 4-inch side. Glue 2 mittens over the end of each wire. Glue folded felt over the wire at edge of mittens.

4 From red felt, cut a circle approximately 11 inches wide; use scissors to shape circle into a cape. From each side of the body, insert wire arms into the middle. Bend wire to position arms as desired. Glue cape onto the top center of body. Glue the doll head onto cape. Embellish body by gluing cotton balls around center of the body (points of folded magazine). Glue cotton batting onto cape edges and around mitten cuffs.

DECORATIVE JAR CANDLE

Using a sheer holiday print fabric, recycle a glass jar into a sparkling accent. Choose a jar about 4 to 5 inches high with an opening of at least 3 inches wide. Or purchase a "jar candle," one with the candle already inside.

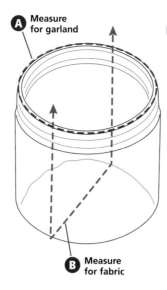

A Measure for garland

B Measure for fabric

1 Measure around lip of jar **(A)**. Measure from lip on one side under the bottom to lip on other side **(B)**. Record measurements. Cut trim about ¼ inch longer than lip measurement. Hot-glue trim to outside lip of jar. If using a garland instead of a trim, cut garland a few inches longer than lip measurement and set aside until step 3.

2 Cut a circle of fabric, 2 to 3 inches larger than the measurement around bottom of jar. Placing fabric flat and wrong side up, place jar in center of fabric.

3 Pull fabric up around jar, and secure with rubber band around fabric and lip of jar. Arrange gathers evenly around rubber band, pulling gathers to be evenly extended from rubber band. If using garland, place around rim; twist ends so garland fits taut, leaving a few inches to arrange decoratively. Make sure garland elements do not extend to the inside of jar. Glue in place at about 3 points around the rim. If not using garland, add appropriate embellishment over "seam" in trim, as a focal point. Place candle inside jar.

2 TRADITIONS

December holidays are built upon a foundation of customs. Enhance your family's **Christmas, Hanukkah** or **Kwanzaa** celebration with one of the wonderful handmade creations offered here. It's time to honor the **Traditions** that make December special.

ADVENT CALENDAR

Hang this Advent calendar full of candy gold coins or dog treats, for 24 days of Christmas spirit for the family. Fabric creates a soft quilted look that is easy to create with minimal sewing skill. Raw edges are intended to fray.

1 Out of "tree" fabric, cut two 3-inch crosswise strips. Cut strips to lengths: 3, 4½, 6, 7½, 9, 10½, 12, and 13½ inches. Press all strips in half lengthwise. Fold each end at diagonal and press. The 3-inch length forms a triangle.

2 Mark lines for stitching, at 1½-inch intervals, starting and ending at the inside corner of diagonal, except for bottom strip. For bottom strip, measure 1¾ inches, forming 2 pockets on each side. Starting with 4½-inch strip (number one), stamp each "pocket" in numerical order.

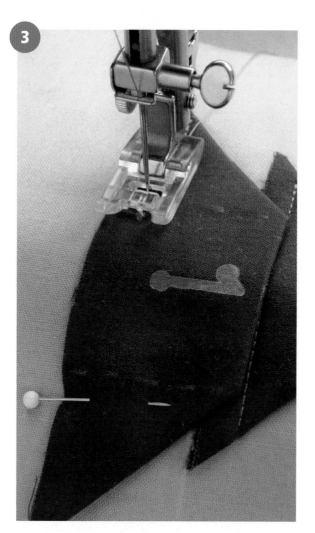

3 Cut background fabric to a 17- by 17-inch square. Cut lining fabric and batting to 17 by 16 inches. Place batting under square of fabric and 1 inch from top edge. Pin. Mark top center and a short parallel line 4½ inches from top. Place raw edge of folded triangle centered along line; pin. Sew along bottom, ¼ inch from raw edge, securing stitching. Continue stitching in order, centering and placing each folded edge along previous stitching. Center "trunk" and tuck into "pocket" of bottom row. Stitch sides. Hand stitch button star to top of tree.

To complete, place lining fabric 1 inch below top of background fabric, right sides together, and pin. Stitch ½-inch seam around sides and bottom. Turn to right side. Fold 1-inch casing at top and stitch along edge. Stitch bells at end of "branches."

PENNY POCKET ORNAMENT

Make this cute pocket ornament from wool in Christmas colors. The penny is for good luck. No machine stitching needed.

1 Make paper pattern for "pocket" by drawing parallel lines 2¼ inches apart and 4 inches long. Draw a line 2¼ inches along length of pattern. Round corners and cut. Use full pattern to pin and cut flap/back. Fold pattern at 2¼-inch line, pin and cut front.

2 Pin "pocket" together. Place flap over front of pocket; use a pin to mark snap placement on flap and pocket front. Follow manufacturer's instructions to affix snap. With 30-inch length of embroidery floss, stitch pocket together with blanket stitch at about ¼-inch intervals and ¼ inch deep. Knot and tuck the beginning piece of floss between pocket pieces. At end, leave about 6 to 8 inches on the inside, knotting near fabric. About ¼ inch from edge, pull thread and needle through to right side. This creates half of loop for hanging.

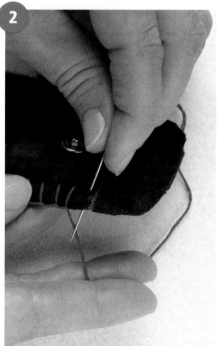

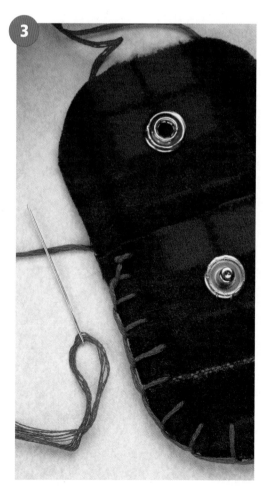

3 From right side of flap (when closed), work blanket stitch around flap edges. Leave 6 to 8 inches of floss at beginning on right side, knotting inside before starting blanket stitch. With both ends of floss and an overhand knot, create loop for hanging. Trim floss even. Place penny in "pocket" for good luck.

FEATHER TREE-TOP ANGEL

This unique feathered angel presents an airy look. Using feathers purchased at a craft store, this simple angel will be the crowning glory of your tree. Personalize as you wish.

MATERIALS

- 18- by 9-inch white or ecru card stock (minimum)
- 1 bag of 4- to 6-inch-long feathers
- 3¼-inch porcelain angel head and arms
- 1 set of feather wings
- 6-inch pearl strand
- 5 inches (¼-inch-wide) white trim
- Small artificial evergreen branch or other embellishment for angel to hold

TOOLS

- Marking pen
- Tape measure
- Tack
- Scissors
- Stapler or tape
- Bottle or jar
- Hot glue gun and glue sticks
- Tweezers or toothpick

$$

1 Using tape measure secured at end, trace a circle on card stock at 9-inch point. Cut circle. Form a cone that overlaps 6 inches; staple or tape. Place cone over bottle. Start adding the longest feathers so they overlap the edge of cone. Place glue on cone at point where base of feather will be. **Tip:** Use tweezers or toothpick to hold feather secure. Encircle cone with feathers. Mark placement of arms and glue them. **Tip:** When gluing heavier items hold them a bit for glue to set.

2 Add head by putting glue on inside and along edges. Place on top of cone and hold in place for a while. Shape wire in wings to fit back of angel; glue in place.

3 Finish placing feathers around arms, shoulders and wings. When adding these feathers, place glue on feather and then add or place among existing feathers. Add feathers evenly around neckline. Add trim to cover this area. Apply glue to trim; put in place. For halo, add a drop of glue to head and place circle of pearls. Add glue to evergreen branch and place in angel's hands. **Tip:** To remove excess tendrils of glue, dissolve using hairdryer.

SHEER TREE SKIRT

Make this elegant tree skirt by piecing together 4 different sheer fabrics. With a finished size of about 28 inches, this sample works well for a tabletop tree. For a larger skirt, simply add more squares.

2 Cut sheer lining the size of pieced top. Right sides together, pin top to lining. Between fabrics and with tassel to inside, pin tassel at each corner. Stitch outer edge at ¼ inch. Pin, mark and cut center hole for tree trunk and a line from hole to center back.

1 Cut three 9½-inch squares of gold; three silver; two red; one white. Arrange with white square at back center. Use a narrow, medium-length zigzag stitch, ¼ inch from edge. Hold thread tails to start seams. Right sides facing, stitch each block together, forming a row of three. Repeat for three rows. Pin rows together, right sides facing, and stitch to form square.

3 Turn right side out, gently pushing out corners and finger pressing edges. Pin raw edge together. Cut 2 pieces of fusible tricot: the length of the straight raw edge and a 30-inch piece for the circle. Fold tricot in half lengthwise, encasing straight edge, and fuse according to manufacturer's directions. Do not allow hot iron to come into too much contact with sheer fabric. Trim tricot even with circle edge. For circle, leave about a 7-inch tail; pin bottom half of tricot under circle. Turn tricot to top side and fuse. Fuse ties lengthwise. At intersections of pieces, sew buttons through both layers.

VICTORIAN-STYLE TREE-SHAPED ORNAMENT

Delicate and elegant, this ornament makes use of natural cotton batting, small pearl or antique buttons and soft-colored roses. It's pretty enough to use with a bow for wrapping packages.

1 Onto two layers of batting, use fabric marker to trace cookie cutter with dots. The dots will be your stitching line. Leaving a generous seam allowance, cut out shape beyond stitching line. For hanging loop, fold ribbon in half, making an overhand knot at end. Sandwich loop between layers at top of tree; pin in place. Pin frequently around tree, especially at curves and points. Stitch on stitching line; at points, pivot (leave needle in batting, picking up presser foot and turning). Do not stitch trunk of tree.

2 Trim about ¼ inch beyond stitching line. Remove dots. Use a chopstick to stuff with fiberfill. Be sure to get stuffing into all areas. Do not stuff trunk; hand stitch around trunk to close.

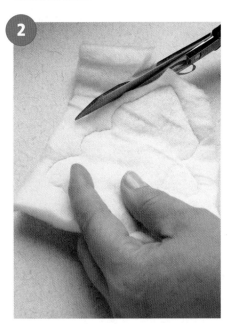

3 Lay out embellishments to determine placement. Cut pearl strand into three unequal lengths. To apply embellishments, start with largest item. Take a stitch into tree center then through back of rose or button. (For illustration purposes, photo shows contrasting thread.) Take another stitch and come out at place for next button or rose. Pull stitch taut. Occasionally, stitch over pearl strand ends to form loops. Continue until all embellishments are added. If needed, glue pearl strands at their base.

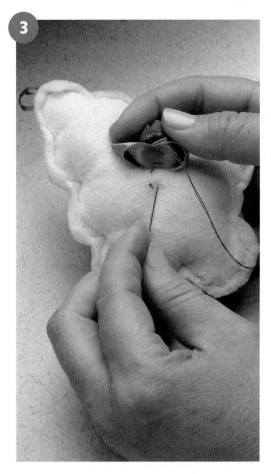

COOKIE CUTTER ORNAMENT

Making use of an antique or new metal cookie cutter, this ornament is also aromatic with the addition of bay leaves and cinnamon sticks. Consider adding other items, such as cranberries or dried orange slices, as well.

42

1 Soak dry cinnamon sticks about ½ hour. Tear—do not cut—fabric into ½-inch strip. Cut strip into two 8- to 10-inch lengths. (An additional length for a final bow is optional.) Form a loop on one end of the wire; add a fabric strip centered on loop. Twist loop around fabric, securing it.

2 Working on a scrap board surface, use an awl to poke holes in the center of bay leaves and cinnamon sticks.

3 Thread wire through a bay leaf group, crisscross a couple cinnamon sticks and fruit, if desired. Repeat. Form a loop at top, similar to beginning loop. Put a fabric strip in and twist to secure. Either cut extra wire or twist it decoratively. To form a hanging loop, make an overhand knot at end of fabric. Tie cookie cutter to bottom. Add a fabric bow at base of hanging loop, if desired.

43

CUSTOMIZED "COOKIES FOR SANTA" PLATE

This is a great child participation project. A child's drawing, decoupaged to the back of a clear plate, serves as this plate's focal point. Since the plate cannot be submerged in water, simply wipe it clean after each use.

MATERIALS

- Clear glass plate
- Child's drawing, including handwritten "Cookies for Santa"
- Decoupage medium
- Sponge applicator
- Paint pen specifically for glass

TOOLS

- Scissors
- Copy machine

$

1 Make a color copy of child's drawing. If necessary, adjust size when photocopying. Cut out drawing in a circle the size of the plate bottom. If the bottom has a ridge, cut circle to fit inside the ridge. Clean plate well with soapy hot water; dry thoroughly. With sponge applicator, apply decoupage medium to front of drawing copy. **Tip:** Work on a protected surface and do not use too much decoupage medium.

2 Immediately apply drawing to bottom of plate. Center and smooth the paper to remove bumps. Check from the right side. With a damp paper towel, remove any decoupage medium overlapping on glass; clean the applicator sponge. Let plate dry. To protect bottom of drawing, apply decoupage medium to bottom of plate over paper. Remove any decoupage medium overlapping on glass and clean applicator sponge.

3 Tape lettering in place on back side of rim. Using paint pen, paint the lettering. Let dry, according to manufacturer's directions. Do not bake the lettering; due to use of decoupage medium, this plate cannot be submerged in water.

POLYMER CLAY ORNAMENT

Create these ornaments using any holiday or theme cookie cutters and Polymer or oven-bake clay. This easy project is perfect for a child's participation; be sure to assist with cutting and baking.

MATERIALS

- 2-ounce package ivory Polymer clay (for bone)
- 2-ounce package green Polymer clay (for tree)
- 2-ounce package red Polymer clay (for tree)
- 3-inch metal or plastic cookie cutters
- Wax paper
- Aluminum foil
- Toothpicks
- 20 inches narrow ribbon or monofilament
- Small star button or bells for embellishments (optional)
- Glossy spray acrylic sealant or special varnish from the clay manufacturer (optional)

TOOLS

- Rolling pin
- Tape
- Knife
- Baking sheet
- Oven & oven mitt

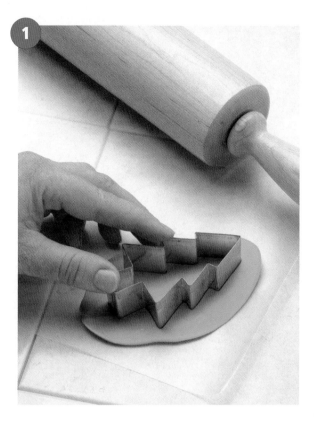

1 Preheat oven to 225°F, or according to manufacturer's directions. For bone ornament, use about ⅓ package; for tree ornament, use about ¼ package. Work into pancake shape in hand; this warms it to make pliable. Roll out on shiny side of wax paper with rolling pin. If clay sticks to rolling pin, wrap aluminum foil, shiny side out, around pin and secure with tape. Roll clay to ⅛ to ¼ inch thick and large enough for cutter; press cutter into clay. If using plastic cookie cutter, gently cut around edge with knife. Peel shape gently from paper, running a knife under edge if necessary. Color will bleed to wax paper, so avoid reusing areas where bleeding has occurred.

2 With toothpick, make a hole for hanging. Handle clay gently, as fingerprints or nicks will show. If desired, use toothpick to add texture to cutout surface.

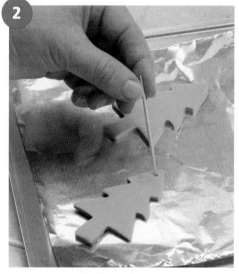

3 From red clay, roll out strips of clay and trim edges straight for bow; roll strips in hands to form "garland" and roll small balls for ornaments. Press gently into place. Cover baking sheet with aluminum foil, shiny side up, and place ornaments on top. Bake according to directions (usually 15 minutes). Let cool and add hanging loop of ribbon or monofilament. If desired, add embellishments and finish with sealant to make shiny.

47

TRADITIONAL CHRISTMAS STOCKING

Add a hint of gold metallic rickrack to make this Christmas stocking glitter. Sewing with felt is quick and easy.

MATERIALS

- 28- by 18-inch burgundy felt (check cut size for felt)
- 9- by 12-inch hunter green felt
- 9- by 12-inch white felt
- 6 yards (½-inch) gold rickrack
- Tailor's chalk or marking pencil
- Burgundy thread
- Dark green thread
- White thread
- 10 inches decorative cording

TOOLS

- Paper scissors
- Shears
- Rotary cutter and mat (optional)
- See-through ruler
- Pins
- Sewing machine

$

1 Enlarge pattern to 15 inches long by 6 inches at cuff (400%). Cut burgundy felt into two 14- by 18-inch pieces; cut green felt into one 6- by 9-inch piece. On burgundy felt, mark 14-inch lines 1½ inches apart. On green felt, mark 6-inch lines 1 inch apart. Cut ten 14-inch pieces of rickrack and eight 6-inch pieces. Pin rickrack on marked lines; with matching thread, stitch down center.

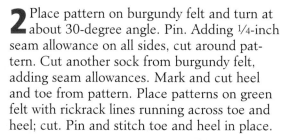

2 Place pattern on burgundy felt and turn at about 30-degree angle. Pin. Adding ¼-inch seam allowance on all sides, cut around pattern. Cut another sock from burgundy felt, adding seam allowances. Mark and cut heel and toe from pattern. Place patterns on green felt with rickrack lines running across toe and heel; cut. Pin and stitch toe and heel in place.

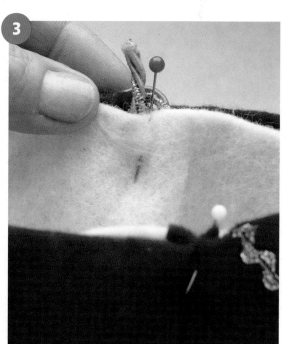

3 Pin sock right sides together and stitch. Turn right side out. Cut cuff 4½ inches deep and the measurement around outside of sock plus ½ inch. Seam cuff, pinning and stitching short edges together to make a circle. Stitch rickrack on one long edge of cuff. Place cuff inside sock, right side of cuff to wrong side of sock, sandwiching 10-inch cording between, with loop facing down; pin and stitch. Turn cuff to right side.

Heel

Toe

SLEIGH BELL ORNAMENT

Paint a large sleigh bell with a simple Christmas or winter scene. Use the bell to adorn the tree or a wreath, or make three to group together on the front door. The designs are freehand, easy and made to look like "folk" art.

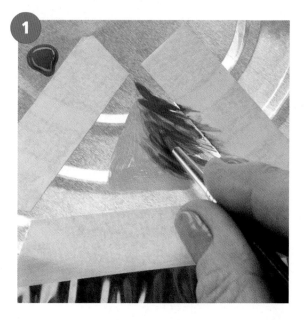

1 Measure design area on bell. First practice the design. On disposable pie tin, use tape to mark an area the same size as design area on bell. Paint a tree: Use flat brush and light green paint to form a triangle. With round brush and medium green, paint branches, extending beyond triangle, but using triangle as a guide. To paint a cabin, paint rectangles for sides; angle roof. With darker brown, fill in sides horizontally to resemble logs. Fill in roof with wavy lines. Add chimney with one stroke of flat brush.

2 Now paint the design on bell: Place bell on coffee mug. Paint designs onto bell as practiced. Allow paint to dry. Go over designs to make them darker and more detailed in the same manner as above. Let dry. If desired, add smaller trees around cabin; let dry.

3 With yellow paint and flat brush, add window glow. With round brush and white paint, add smoke from chimney and snow along roofline and on some branches. With a slightly damp sponge, apply white paint to create snow-covered ground. If desired, sign and date your creation. Add ribbon and tie in loop.

DECORATIVE TABLETOP TREE

Multiply your holiday spirit by displaying more than one decorated tree during the holidays! Place a tabletop tree on a sideboard, sofa table, in a child's room or in the family room. Let color determine your theme, or decorate with children's work, ethnic objects or antique trinkets. On this decorative tree, frosted or dried fruit could add depth and interest.

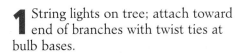

1 String lights on tree; attach toward end of branches with twist ties at bulb bases.

2 Attach holly floral picks with twist ties and fasten balls in place toward end of branches.

3 Using twist ties, attach larger floral picks to top of tree. Using about 15 feet of ribbon, wrap it around picks, covering stems; tie a large bow, then wrap long ends of ribbon as garland throughout tree. Tie another length of ribbon at top of tree; wrap around and down the tree. Cut blossom stems to about 10 inches; for closer to treetop, cut a few shorter blossoms. Tuck larger blossoms into tree as focal points.

EVERLASTING MISTLETOE BALL

Make this mistletoe ball from artificial leaves and beads to represent the berries. The beads and copper wire give it sparkle. Unlike a ball made from real mistletoe berries, this ball will last and is not toxic to children and pets.

MATERIALS

- 4-inch green styrofoam ball
- 5 yards (¼-inch) red ribbon
- 3½ yards (¼-inch) red/metallic ribbon (optional)
- 1 or more mistletoe bushes
- 28 white/iridescent beads
- 22-gauge copper wire, approximately 10 feet

TOOLS

- Pins or florist pins
- Scissors
- Hot glue gun and glue sticks
- Wire cutters
- Needle-nose pliers

$$

1 Cut red ribbon: two 60-inch lengths; two 30-inch lengths. Cut metallic ribbon: four 30-inch lengths. Crisscross centers of two 60-inch lengths; pin to ball. This becomes the bottom. Bring ribbons to top and pin, dividing ball into quarters.

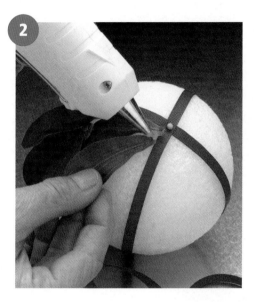

2 Add leaves from mistletoe bush: Start at either top or bottom and complete one quarter at a time. For each leaf, place a dot of glue on ball and apply leaf. Leaves may be sparse at this step. Let ribbon show in areas.

3 Measure and cut 28 3-inch pieces of wire. Twist one end of wire around tip of pliers. On opposite end, thread bead and use pliers to twist wire around bead. Hang ball in a working area and insert wires randomly into styrofoam. Cover bare spaces with additional leaves by dotting glue onto base of leaf then applying leaf to ball. **Tip:** Use hair dryer to dissolve glue tendrils. Insert red, 30-inch ribbon, at base of ball. Tie top and bottom ribbons, each in an overhand knot near ball. Add metallic ribbon at top and bottom, if desired.

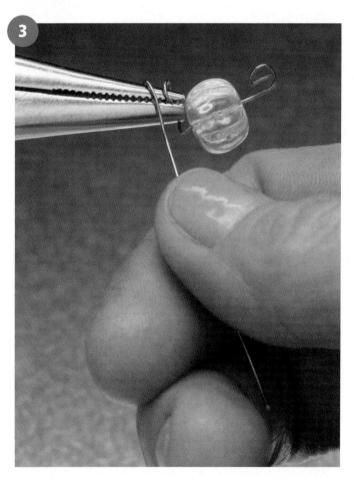

PIXIE ORNAMENTS

Create the bodies of these cute little ornaments from a variety of items, including bells, blossoms or pinecones. These are also perfect gift toppers. Plan to make many!

MATERIALS

- ¾-inch knob head
- 1 small package doll hair
- Black marking or paint pen
- Red marking or paint pen
- Red felt scraps
- Green felt scraps
- Red thread
- 6-mm jingle bell
- 1¼-inch-high bell or 1½-inch-high blossom or pinecone (for body)
- Narrow, thin red ribbon
- Small embellishment (for front of cape)

TOOLS

- Toothpicks
- Styrofoam block
- Clear tape
- Paper
- Shears and scissors
- Hot glue gun and glue sticks
- Hand sewing needle

$

1 With black marking pen, make dot eyes and mouth. (Between tasks, set knob head on toothpick in styrofoam.) Cut short lengths of doll hair; stick onto 1-inch length of tape, grouping hair strands toward middle of tape and covering ½ inch. **Tip:** Work with longer strands and trim later. Cut tape in half lengthwise and tape in place on head. Trim as desired.

2 On paper, sketch a 2-inch half circle for hat pattern; use pattern to cut hat from red felt. Thread needle and tie knot in end of double strand. Loop thread through bell. Fold straight edges of hat together, forming cone. Stitch into hat tip, pulling bell to top; hand stitch down the straight edge, then tie knot. Trim hat edge in front, if needed. Glue hat to head.

3 Glue head to body. Cut an 8-inch piece of ribbon and tie ends together to form loop. Attach ribbon to pixie's neck, with loop to back.

4 On paper, sketch a 3-inch half circle for cape pattern; use pattern to cut cape from red felt. From green felt, cut 1½- by ¼-inch rectangle. Glue cape around body. Glue scarf with ends extending to one side. Cut fringe in scarf. Glue embellishment onto front of cape.

FAST AND EASY TREE SKIRT

This unique and fun polar fleece tree skirt requires a little sewing and lots of cutting. Great for a tabletop tree, this 30-inch tree skirt can easily be adapted to fit a larger tree; simply lengthen the radius of circle when making the pattern.

MATERIALS

- Tissue paper
- 1 yard (60-inch-wide) polar fleece
- Matching thread

TOOLS

- Newspaper
- Tape measure and tack
- Marking pen
- See-through ruler (optional)
- Tape
- Scissors
- Pins
- Shears, rotary cutter and cutting mat (optional)
- Sewing machine

1 Make first part of pattern by tracing ¼ of a circle on newspaper: Tack the very end of measuring tape to corner of paper and move tape measure in arc marking 15 inches. Cut out pattern. Fold in half, making ⅛ of a circle.

2 Place newspaper on tissue: tape down to secure. Mark around newspaper pattern. Add 2 inches to all straight lines. The original straight line is the stitching line.

3 Place tissue pattern on double thickness of fabric with wrong sides together. Pin and cut. Repeat three more times.

4 With wrong sides together and starting at small end, sew a seam, two inches from edge. Stop stitching 2 inches from end; secure stitches. **Tip:** Use tape to mark 2 inches on sewing machine for guidance. Pin, wrong sides together, next piece. Repeat until one seam is left. Do not sew this.

5 Place seam flat on cutting surface and cut fringe to about ¼ inch from stitching. Stop cutting where stitching ends and cut out a square measuring about 2 by 2 inches. Continue with all seams. Fringe unstitched open ends.

6 Open up skirt; place pattern in one section, 2 inches from rounded edge; pin. Cut fringe to pattern. Repeat for each section. Use top fringes on open ends to tie tree skirt in place. Arrange fringes randomly.

FAST AND EASY STOCKING

Make this simple stocking in less than an hour. Using polar fleece and a fun holiday or theme print is key. Personalize the cuff with stitched-on letters.

MATERIALS

- Pattern (from Traditional Christmas Stocking on page 48 or a commercial one measuring about 14 inches high and 7 inches at cuff)
- Polar fleece print, 15 inches if directional (as shown) or 12 inches if not
- Polar fleece, 6 inches of a coordinating solid color
- 6 inches (¼-inch) cording or ribbon
- Matching thread

TOOLS

- Shears
- Rotary cutter and cutting mat (optional)
- Pins
- Tape measure
- Sewing machine

$

1 If using pattern from Traditional Christmas Stocking increase the width a bit and shorten pattern by 1 inch. Place pattern on double thickness of fabric. If the design is directional, place pattern to be consistent. Cut 2 stockings. Using ¼-inch seam, stitch front straight seam only, right sides together. Spread stocking open and measure width of top (where cuff will go). From coordinating fabric, cut cuff fabric to width of top by 4½ inches long.

2 Pin cuff to wrong side of stocking and stitch, using ½-inch seam allowance. Pin seam allowance toward bottom of stocking and stitch ¼ from seam to hold seam allowances in place.

3 Pin sock and cuff, right sides together. Place ribbon loop just above seam in cuff and pin between pieces of fabric. Stitch, using ¼-inch seam allowance around rest of sock, stopping just past loop. Leave rest of cuff open. Turn to right side and cut fringe every ½ inch and into cuff 2½ to 3 inches. If desired, add name to upper part of cuff before stitching. When cutting fringe, cut fringe to below name.

MENORAH FOR LITTLE HANDS

This is a very simple menorah that the kids can help make then decorate to their hearts' content. Cutting, painting and using the glue gun require handling by an adult. By making it for 7 candles, it can be used as a kinara for Kwanzaa celebrations.

MATERIALS

- 1x4 or 1x3 wood board, 20 inches long
- Wood glue
- Aerosol paint, blue (or desired color)
- 9 (3/8-inch) nuts
- 1½- to 2-inch Star of David stamp (or other design)
- White glue
- Glitter

TOOLS

- Measuring tape or ruler
- Saw
- Sandpaper
- Hot glue gun and glue sticks
- Small brush

$

1 Cut board into 18-inch and 1½-inch lengths. Sand edges lightly. Using wood glue, glue 1½-inch length to center of longer board. Let dry about 1 hour. Spray paint. When paint is dry sand edges for an antiqued look, if desired.

2 For placement of nuts, mark the center of the small block of wood. Measure 1 inch from edge of small block of wood, centered (on larger piece of wood) and mark. Continue marking 1½ inches apart until 4 marks are on each side of center.

3 Work on a paper-protected surface for easier cleanup. Add designs at end of board, by brushing white glue sparingly on stamp and placing it on board. Remove stamp and shake glitter over glue. Let dry. Rinse brush and stamp immediately. Gently shake off excess glitter. To glue nuts in place, apply hot glue to bottom of nut; place nut on mark. Let dry.

HANUKKAH BANNER

This fabric Hanukkah banner requires minimal sewing skills. Letters are made from fabric and paper-backed fusible web. Letters could also be stamped as in the Kwanzaa Door Sign (page 72) or stenciled.

MATERIALS

- ⅓ yard cotton quilting (main fabric)
- 2 inches contrasting firmly woven cotton quilting (for letters)
- 1-inch strip alphabet to trace
- 4 inches paper-backed fusible web
- Quilting tracing pencil
- ⅓ yard thin cotton batting
- Matching thread
- Ribbon for hanging, approximately 20 inches
- 10½-inch-long (⅛- to ¼-inch) dowel for hanging

TOOLS

- Iron
- Shears
- Sewing machine

$

1 Keeping paper and fusible web together, fuse to wrong side of fabric for letters. Layer as follows, from top: Fabric, right side up; web; paper. Trace letters onto right side of fabric. Cut out letters. Remove paper from letters.

2 Cut main fabric to a 10- by 37½-inch rectangle. (This piece will be both front and back of banner.) Cut batting to 10 by 17¼ inches. On right side of fabric, align letters. Start about 3 inches from top and go down about 14 inches. Fuse letters to fabric. Fold right sides of main fabric together, extending front by about 1½ inches. Place batting on fabric and pin. Using ½-inch seam allowance, sew along both long edges.

3 Turn fabric right sides out and poke out corners. Fold ½ inch to wrong side on extended fabric at top; press. Turn extended fabric to back, about 1 inch; pin. Stitch along top edge to create a casing for dowel. Place dowel in casing; use ribbon to hang.

DREIDEL FOR HANUKKAH GAMES

Make this wooden dreidel from a purchased 1½-inch-square piece of wood. Add the Hebrew letters Nun, Gimmel, Heh and Shin freehand or by tracing them and coloring them in. Have fun playing!

DREIDEL RULES

Most people play dreidel for chocolate coins, matchsticks or pennies. The Hebrew letters stand for the phrase "Nes Gadol Hayah Sham," a great miracle happened there, referring to the miracle of the oil. The letters also stand for the Yiddish words nit (nothing), gantz (all), halb (half) and shtell (put), which represent dreidel's basic rules. To start, each player puts in one coin. A player spins the dreidel. On Nun, nothing happens; on Gimmel, you win the whole pot; on Heh, you win half of the pot; and on Shin, you put one in. When the pot is empty, everybody puts one in. Keep playing until one person has everything. Then redivide it, because nobody likes a poor winner.

MATERIALS

- 1½x1½ pine or other soft wood (actual measurements are 1¼ inches square)
- 1-inch length of (¼-inch-diameter or less) dowel
- Wood glue
- Sandpaper
- Graphite tracing paper (optional)
- Permanent marking pen or oil pencils
- Aerosol sealant in matte finish

TOOLS

- Ruler and pencil
- Drill and bit to match dowel size
- Miter box and saw or electric miter saw

1 Cut piece of wood 2 inches long. Mark one end with diagonal lines from each corner, to form an X. Drill hole at center of X about ½ inch deep. This becomes the top.

2 Mark the halfway point on one bottom cut edge. To easily do this, cut a piece of paper the width measurement and fold in half to get center. Cut a 45-degree angle from center mark to outside edge. Cut the opposite side the same way to form a point.

3 Mark the halfway point on the tip, using the above paper method. Cut a 45-degree angle from center mark to outside edge. Cut the opposite side the same way to form a point. Cut dowel to 1 inch. Put glue on end of dowel and insert into hole. Sand edges lightly. Add the appropriate letters, by tracing them with graphite paper, or do freehand. Color them in with a permanent marking pen or oil pencil. Spray with acrylic sealant.

Nun

Gimmel

Heh

Shin

STAR OF DAVID PLACEMAT

Use a purchased placemat or one you make as a base for this project. Ribbon Stars of David are easy to make, and the entire project can be done without machine sewing. Add as many stars as desired or make a table runner.

MATERIALS

- White, silver or blue placemat
- ½-inch-wide ribbon, 30 inches for each star
- Fusible web scraps
- Matching thread
- Hand sewing needle
- 6 medium beads and 12 seed beads or small buttons (optional) for each star

TOOLS

- Paper, ruler, pencil and scissors (for pattern)
- Shears
- Iron and ironing board

$

1 Steam-shrink ribbon by ironing it with a medium/steam setting. On paper, create pattern for triangle with 3 equal sides of 3½ inches; cut out pattern. Tape triangle to ironing board surface. Starting in lower right corner, place ribbon on outside edge of triangle. Leave ¼-inch extension of ribbon. Pin. At next point of triangle, turn ribbon, keeping edge along outside of triangle and pin at point. Continue until back to beginning. To finish, turn ribbon as if it were continuing around triangle, lining it up with beginning piece of ribbon. Press using medium hot iron. Trim tail of beginning ribbon at an angle to tuck into fold. Trim away any extra ribbon. Using tiny piece of fusible web, fuse the overlap of the ribbons. Press at points. Make another ribbon triangle.

2 Invert one triangle over the other and adjust to make the points equal, about an inch. Using a small piece of fusible web, fuse at intersections. **Tip:** Use tip of pin to insert the piece of fusible web between layers.

3 Position star on placemat, as desired and, using several small pieces of fusible web, fuse to hold temporarily in place. Using needle and thread, sew a bead or beads or a button at each intersection. (Photo shows contrasting colored thread to illustrate technique.)

STAR OF DAVID IN LIGHTS

Create this outdoor, 24-inch sparkling Star of David from purchased wood and strings of blue and white lights. Make it smaller, larger or make it all blue or all white.

MATERIALS

- 2 (8-foot) 1x2 pieces of lumber
- Wood glue
- 12 brads
- 6 (1½-inch-long) wood screws
- 2 eyelet screws
- 24 inches (24-gauge) wire
- White and blue spray paint (use just one color if desired)
- Mini-light strings, 50 lights each of white and blue (with lights at 2- to 3-inch intervals)

TOOLS

- Radial-arm saw
- Protractor or adjustable T square
- Ruler
- Strap (adjustable if possible)
- Hammer
- Drill and ¼-inch bit
- Heavy-duty staple gun with long staples and twist ties (optional)

$

1 Cut six 24-inch lengths from 1x2s. Mark 30-degree angle at end of each piece, keeping length at 24 inches. Set up saw to follow this line; do not follow degree markings on saw. When saw is set up for correct angle, add a block clamped in place where end of board can always be placed for cutting. Make a couple practice cuts to make sure angles will create triangle.

2 Place 3 cut boards in triangle and line up seams. Glue, and encircle with strap, pull tight and let dry. Put brads 1½ inches from tip. Repeat for other triangle. Place one triangle on top of other, inversed, to form star. Make sure star points are equal. Drill holes at intersections. Screw in place. On back side of top horizontal board, drill holes about 6 inches from tips. Place eyelet screws for hanging.

3 Start placing lights at bottom tip, wrapping the cord around outside of triangle. Staple over cord periodically as you go, taking care not to staple into cord. Hold lights in place temporarily with twist ties. Hold wood on a solid surface. Line and staple lights to inside of triangle. Put blue lights on one triangle and white lights on the other. If you have extra lights, hang them down from star and intertwine.

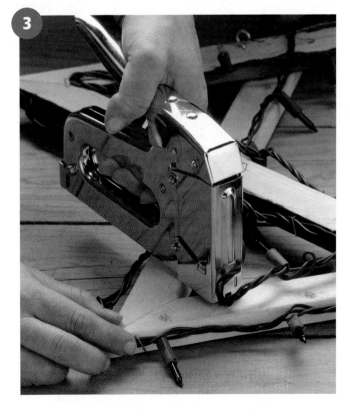

KWANZAA DOOR SIGN

Make a Kwanzaa door sign or banner out of batik-looking fabric with stamped, stenciled or fused letters. Choose whimsical letters and stamping to fit with the batik-look. Hang bells from the bottom to make noise upon entry.

1 Cut fabric to 8 by 28 inches. Cut interfacing to 7 by 27 inches. Place fabric on protected work surface. To get a light even coating on stamp, use brush to apply paint to stamp. Centered on lower half of fabric, vertically stamp letters for "KWANZAA" and let dry. Press fabric to set paint following manufacturer's instructions. Following manufacturer's instructions, fuse interfacing to wrong side of fabric, leaving ½ inch of fabric extended on all sides.

2 Fold extended fabric over interfacing and press. Place fusible web strips along two long sides, 1 inch short of halfway point. Pin, with pin heads extending beyond fabric. Fold in half, lining up edges and press to fuse, following manufacturer's instructions. **Tip:** With tip of iron, fuse between pins, then remove pins and finish fusing.

3 Cut two web strips: one 6 and one 2 inches long. Place 6-inch strip inside open area at bottom of hanging. Cut two 3-inch strips of leather. Fold each in half and place bell in each. Sandwich leather strips between a small strip of fusible interfacing and fuse to hold together. Place at center and between fabric pieces with 2-inch web strip on top of them. Fuse. Place dowel through opening at top. To hang sign, tie 12-inch leather strip around each dowel end.

KWANZAA CELEBRATION MAT

Part of the Kwanzaa celebration is to gather the candles and Unity cup on a straw mat. This mat is made from paper ribbon to simulate straw and is an easy-to-do family project.

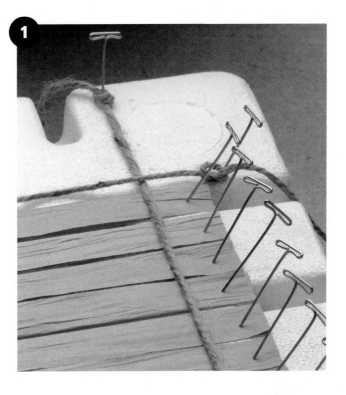

1 Cut 11 tan paper strips 15 inches long. Cut 2 tan and 13 straw paper strips 11½ inches long. Fold in half lengthwise. Cut two 30-inch and two 35-inch lengths of jute. On styrofoam, place tan strips lengthwise, pinning at top. (You will be working from the back side of the mat.) Place one short length of jute about 1 inch below strip ends and across top, attaching to pins with knot. Place the two long lengths of jute along long sides and parallel at about 9 inches. Tie in place.

2 Weave first row with tan strip, going under one, over one and under jute at both ends. Weave next row with straw strip, going over one under one, and under jute at both ends.

3 Weave until mat measures about 13 inches. Place short length of jute over lengthwise strips and near last horizontal strip. Tie as above. Even out weaving if necessary and double check measurements. Pin as needed. Secure ends by starting with the ones that end under a strip. Fold at jute and glue. Hold with clothespin. Glue remaining strips, folding them over jute. Let dry overnight. At each corner, add 2 wooden beads and knot.

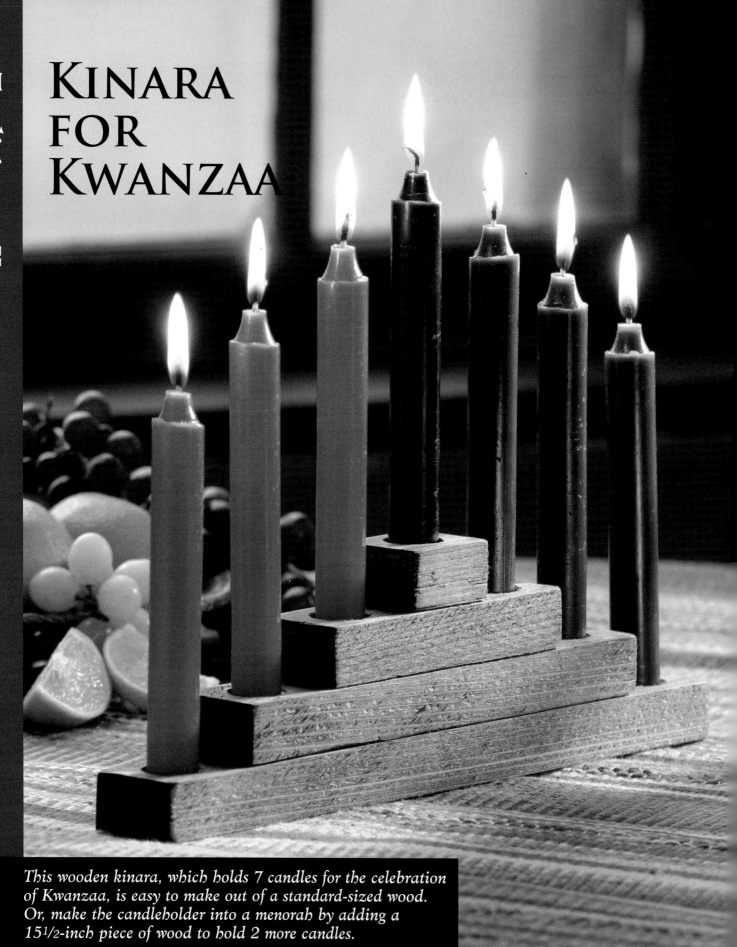

KINARA FOR KWANZAA

This wooden kinara, which holds 7 candles for the celebration of Kwanzaa, is easy to make out of a standard-sized wood. Or, make the candleholder into a menorah by adding a 15½-inch piece of wood to hold 2 more candles.

MATERIALS

- Cedar 1x2 board, 36 inches long
- 8 (1¼-inch) wood screws
- Wood stain (optional)
- Clear aerosol sealant (optional)
- Felt scraps or wax paper

TOOLS

- Hand saw, radial saw or miter saw
- Drill or drill press
- ⅞-inch wood bore bit
- Sandpaper
- ⅛-inch drill bit for pilot holes
- Screwdriver

$

1 On cedar 1x2, measure and mark the following lengths: 1¾, 5¼, 8¾, 12¼ inches. On smallest piece mark the center of that area. (It should be ⅞ inch in from mark or end and ¾ inch from long edges.) Mark the same distance in from each end mark and from edges on the other lengths. At these marks, drill ⅞-inch holes about ½ inch deep. (It is easier to drill the holes before the piece is cut.)

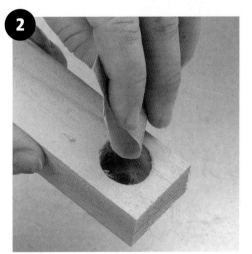

2 Use saw to cut measured lengths apart. Lightly sand all edges, including holes.

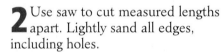

3 Center smallest piece over the next sized piece, candle holes up. From bottom, use ⅛-inch bit to drill 2 pilot holes at about 2 inches from ends and through to smaller piece. Put a screw in each hole and tighten. Continue for the last two pieces, completing the largest piece last. Stain if desired. Finish with a couple coats of clear aerosol sealant, if desired. Line inside of each candle hole with felt or wax paper so candle fits snugly.

KWANZAA PLACEMAT AND NAPKIN RING

Part of any celebration is eating, so make this place setting in colors that reflect the Kwanzaa celebration. Beading is fun, and starting from purchased placemats makes this project easy. Or, change the beads to Christmas colors and make this placemat for Christmas.

1 Cut a length of beading string that is four times the length of the mat's short edge. Thread beading string into needle; double the strand. Mark center of mat's short edge for later reference. Begin stitching: Take a stitch at corner on back of mat, ¼ inch from each edge and through to front. String beads, alternating 2 black and 1 red, until just short of middle.

2 Take a stitch the length of the larger bead into mat and come up near the last small bead. (Photo shows contrasting thread to illustrate.) Add large bead and stitch through mat bringing thread up to where next small bead will start. Add beads as described in Step 1. Stitch through mat to back; take another stitch and tie.

3 Do the same for the other row of beads, starting ¼ inch from first row and alternating with green beads. Go through large bead and continue. To hold lines of beads in place, from the back, stitch up and over strings, every couple inches.

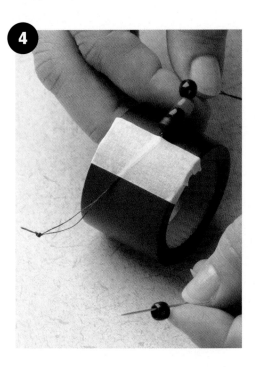

4 **Add beads to napkin ring:** Tape double thread with about a 3-inch tail; knot a couple times where beads will start. String beads as for placemat. With about 1 inch left, double knot and tie thread tails together, stretching thread a bit to tighten. Repeat for second row. The space between the start and end of beads will make the ring stable.

KWANZAA MEMORY ALBUM

Kwanzaa includes gathering family memories and setting goals. Keep them in this artistically covered album that can be personalized in many ways. Sign and date the inside of the album.

1 Measure front cover of album. Cut placemat ¾ inch larger than width and about 3 inches larger than the height. Zigzag or serge cut edges if the fabric tends to ravel. Cut a piece of fusible web to height measurement. Fold spine edge of mat 1 inch; press. Place cording centered and fusible web under fold and fuse according to manufacturer's directions.

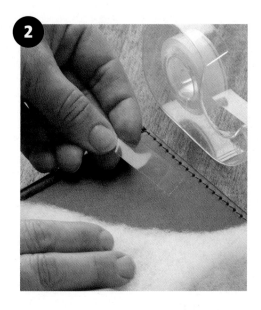

2 Cut a piece of batting about ½ inch smaller on all sides than the cover. Glue or use double-stick tape to adhere batting to cover. Lastly, add additional items to edges or tassel.

3 Position placemat over batting with fused edge next to spine. Pull top and bottom edges taut to inside of cover; hold in place with clothespins or tape. Glue edges down; hold in place with clothespins while drying. Tie cording tautly with a square knot inside front cover. Make tassels from the fringe of the placemat and cover with beads or use purchased tassels and add as desired. You may choose to embellish with additional beads or buttons.

3
WINTER WONDERLAND

The holidays are fun, but winter is outstanding in itself. Bright sunshine and crisp winter skies become backdrops for a beautiful wreath, colorful stars or sparkling light projects as you create your own **Winter Wonderland.**

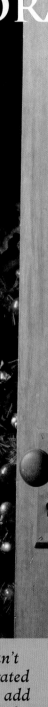
LET IT SNOW DOOR DECORATION

Celebrate what you can't change with this decorated snow shovel created to add fun to your frosty front door.

MATERIALS

- Snow shovel
- Purchased holiday ribbon
- Plastic decorative snowflakes
- Plastic evergreens
- Craft foam:
    White
    Black
    Orange
    Red
    Blue
    Green
- Spray paint (colors depend on your shovel color)
- 2-inch adhesive letters
- Matte finish, clear craft spray

TOOLS

- Hot glue gun and glue sticks
- Painter's tape

$$$

SPRAY PAINT CHOICES

The shovel used in this project had a red handle and a black plastic shovel surface. To achieve a peppermint design cascading down the handle, the crafter applied 2-inch painter's tape to the handle and spray-painted the handle white. Removing the tape reveals the peppermint pattern. The crafter applied 2-inch adhesive letters to the black shovel surface and then spray-painted the entire surface blue. Removing the adhesive letters makes them black against the blue shovel surface. Choose spray paint colors that coordinate and complement the shovel you use. You may use a child-sized shovel for this project.

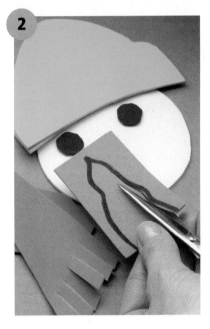

1 **For snowmen:** From white craft foam, cut 2 circles about an inch wider than ribbon width.

2 **For hats, eyes and mouths, carrots and scarves:** From colored craft foam, cut free-form shapes. Hot-glue shapes onto the white circles. For added dimension (for example, hat rim and scarf knot), layer shapes of the same color, and apply with glue.

3 Hot-glue the back of snowmen to the front of ribbon. Attach ribbon to shovel handle with wire or ribbon provided. Hot-glue artificial greens around the ribbon. Then hot-glue plastic snowflakes in and around the ribbon.

4 Using white acrylic paint, dab on "snow" to the tops of the letters on the shovel.

5 When the shovel is dry, spray the entire surface of the shovel with a clear matte finish spray.

Craft tip: Hot glue, low temp glue, and glue specially formulated for craft foam can all be used for this project. Always be extremely careful when using hot glue, and always supervise children.

STAINED-GLASS STARS

Ready to hang outdoors or in, these festive stars are crafted from mulberry paper and allow holiday lights to shine through.

- 12-inch squares of black card stock
- Mulberry paper in assorted colors
- Cord, ball chain or thread

TOOLS

- Copy machine
- Protective cutting mat
- Ruler
- Craft knife
- Scissors
- Laminating plastic or access to a professional laminator (the service is available at many copy shops)
- Paper punch

1 Enlarge patterns at right to full size (300%) and make one copy for each desired star.

2 Place protective cutting mat on work surface. Place black card stock on cutting mat; place desired star pattern on top. Use a ruler and craft knife to cut along each pattern line, being careful not to cut beyond the lines, as shown in photo.

3 Use the cut-away shapes as patterns to cut mulberry paper, cutting with scissors slightly beyond edge of black pattern shape as shown in photo. You can make the stars one color or make each shape within the star a different color.

4 Arrange star pieces and laminate them following manufacturer's instructions as shown in photo. Or, take them to a copy shop to have them professionally laminated.

5 Punch a hole in the point of each star and hang it by cord, ball chain or thread.

JINGLE-JANGLE JESTER SOCK

Make a whimsical front door welcome with a brightly painted canvas stocking that's as easy as painting by number.

MATERIALS

- 1/2 yard of primed artists' canvas
- Acrylic paints:
  - Black
  - Light green
  - Medium green
  - Red
  - Bright pink
  - Purple
  - Light blue
  - Gold
- Black thread
- Red thread
- Plastic bags
- Water-based exterior brush-on varnish
- Various sizes of jingle bells in red and silver

TOOLS

- Pencil
- Paper for patterns
- Scissors
- Small round paintbrush
- 1/2-inch flat paintbrush
- Sewing machine
- Sewing needle

$$

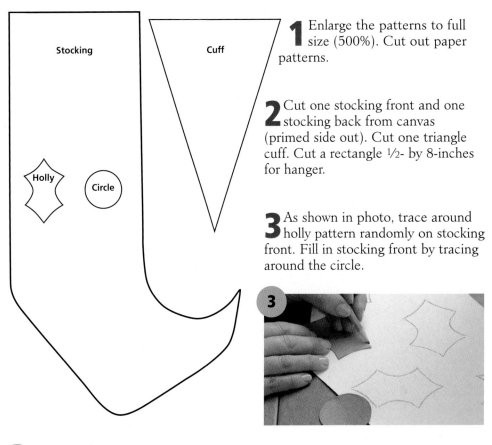

1 Enlarge the patterns to full size (500%). Cut out paper patterns.

2 Cut one stocking front and one stocking back from canvas (primed side out). Cut one triangle cuff. Cut a rectangle 1/2- by 8-inches for hanger.

3 As shown in photo, trace around holly pattern randomly on stocking front. Fill in stocking front by tracing around the circle.

4 Using black paint and a small round brush, paint over lines as shown in photo; let dry.

5 Blending green paints as shown in photo, paint holly. Fill in circles and the hanging strip blending red and bright pink. Paint in the background blending purple and light blue. Paint the triangle gold; blend in red around the edges. Paint the stocking back with a blending of purple and blue. Let dry.

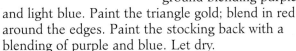

6 Arrange cuff on stocking front. Using a zigzag stitch, machine stitch along the top, 1/8 inch from edge. Fold the hanging strip in half lengthwise; zigzag the center. Stitch the stocking front to back, tucking the hanger ends in the upper right corner.

7 Stuff stocking with plastic bags, then paint stocking back with varnish. Let dry. Turn cuff and brush varnish on stocking front. Let dry. Turn down cuff and varnish. Let dry.

8 Sew desired jingle bells along cuff edge and near hanger.

STAR DOOR HANGER

Using a purchased irregular-shaped wood star as the base, add a metal shape, bells and small dried items, for this decorative hanger. Perfect for the porch door or an inside doorknob, this hanger is not weather-proof for an outside exposed door.

MATERIALS

- 12-inch irregular-shaped wooden star
- Yellow-gold acrylic craft paint
- 5-inch white distressed metal (for contrast), heart shape (or other shape)
- Large button (to give dimension)
- Scrap board
- 1 thick or a few thin pieces of 36-inch raffia
- Small dried items
- Rustic wire for hanging
- Rustic jingle bells

TOOLS

- Paintbrush
- Sandpaper
- Hammer
- Awl
- Drill and bit (large enough for wire to go through)
- Large-eyed needle

$

1 Paint star, leaving some irregularity in the painting. Let dry. Lightly sand edges for a worn look.

2 Position metal heart on star to determine final placement. Position button where you want raffia to come through; mark hole. Place heart on scrap board and punch holes for button. Return heart to position on star; mark holes' placement on star. Drill holes, working on scrap board. Also drill one hole in star's top point for hanging.

3 Thread raffia through needle. Place button over holes in star and place metal heart over button. Align holes. From front, thread raffia through one hole, leaving a tail about half the length of raffia. Thread through other hole from back. Place dried items in place; tie raffia around them. Tie raffia in bow. Trim raffia to desired length. Place rustic wire through top hole, twisting to hold in place; add rustic bells to wire ends.

RUSTIC DOOR SIGN

Glad Tidings

Make this tin square into a rustic sign for the door, to greet your holiday guests. You can choose any message or design. To make it rustic, spatter with paint and add rustic bells with copper wire.

1 Using awl, scrap wood and hammer, pound one hole in each corner of tin square, except in what will be the top corner. At top corner, make two holes 1½ inches from top corner.

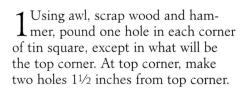

2 Tape border stencil so design is about ½ inch from center design square. Using medium green paint with dauber or stencil brush, apply paint to leaf part of stencil. Dab paint on paper plate to make sure paint is not too thick. Let border dry. Add a motif to lower corner in the same manner. Center greeting stencil; tape to square. Apply white paint and let dry.

3 Cover center design square with paper towel; spatter outside border with white paint by pulling stick across toothbrush dipped in paint. **Tip:** To avoid paint buildup, clean stick after a couple swipes. With red dimensional paint, add berries on holly design. Cut one 12-inch and three 6-inch pieces of wire. Attach 6-inch piece to each bell; twist. If using marble, wrap wire around marble. Attach bells to side holes; twist wire around point to protect point. Add marble or bell to bottom point. Insert 12-inch wire through top two holes; twist to secure.

93

THE SEASON'S STAR

The Season's Star will guide family and friends into your home for the holidays. Shape nature's materials into a glittering festive star by adding your own creative inspiration.

1 Determine size of overall star decoration. Use garden pruner to cut dogwood branches to this measurement. For a five-point star, you will need 15 cut dogwood sticks. Divide cut sticks in groups of three. Place on flat surface, making a V shape with two groups of three sticks each. At a right angle over first V shape, place another V shape with two more groups of three sticks each. You now have three points of a star. Position the remaining three sticks over the V pattern to connect the final two points.

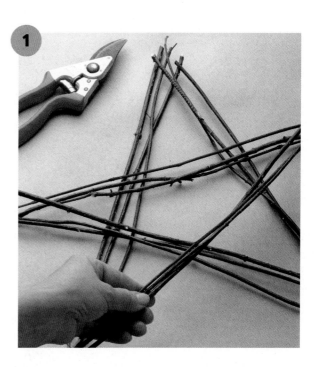

2 Cut wire into five 6-inch pieces. Wrap each piece of wire around one point of the star, twisting wire ends together to secure the sticks. Repeat for four remaining star points. Cut raffia ribbon into five 12-inch pieces. Wrap and tie over wire-wrapped point ends. Tie off with a knot, and even out ends by cutting with scissors.

3 Lay out pinecones and dried flowers to paint with glitter glue. Apply glitter glue to both inside and outside edges. Paint front side of holly leaves with glitter glue; allow to dry.

4 Gather glittered objects along with pine branch. Arrange on top of dogwood star. Use small pieces of wire to attach glittered objects to star. Tie raffia ribbon on as the finishing touch.

RECYCLED PORCH WREATH

Turn a tired old artificial evergreen wreath into a sparkling beauty for your porch. The secret is in grouping the lights in threes and the Christmas balls in twos or threes. You will be surprised at your creation from a can of spray paint, lights and recycled Christmas balls.

- 24-inch old artificial evergreen wreath
- Aerosol paint (silver, pewter or gold)
- String of 35 to 50 mini-lights
- 18 to 20 old Christmas balls
- About 50 twist ties
- A few inches of wire for hanging

TOOLS

- Glue gun and glue sticks

$

1 Spray wreath with paint to the amount of coverage desired. Let dry.

2 Group lights in threes; secure with twist ties at bases. Starting at bottom of wreath, add lights from behind, pushing them through to the front as far as desired. When all lights are in place, plug them in and tweek as desired. Hold wires in place on back of wreath with twist ties attached to wire wreath base.

3 To avoid losing wire-loop caps, hot-glue the caps onto the balls. Determine placement of Christmas balls on wreath, grouping in twos or threes and some individually. Hold each ball group together by threading a twist tie through hangers and twisting in place toward tie's end. When positioning balls in place, thread twist tie through to back of wreath; twist around wreath base to hold. Use some single balls to fill in. Add wire to top for hanging.

SHINING STAR

Make an easy wood star for outdoors or the porch. The star is to appear a bit rustic, made with wire and metallic spray paint. It can be made in sizes from 24 to 36 inches.

MATERIALS

- 1½- by ¾-inch wood board (lattice molding):
    - 15 feet for 36-inch star or
    - 10 feet for 24-inch star
- White paint primer
- Metallic silver spray paint
- 5-foot length (22-gauge) galvanized wire
- Scrap board

TOOLS

- Saw
- Drill with about a ⁵⁄₃₂ bit
- Wire cutters
- Sandpaper (optional)

$

1 Measure and cut boards into 5 pieces to desired length. On each board end, drill hole ½ inch from edge. **Tip:** Place scrap board under drilling. Paint with primer and let dry. Spray with metallic silver, gently and irregularly covering surfaces. Let dry. To make more rustic, sand some of edges to allow white paint and wood to show through, if desired.

2 Position boards on large surface and arrange in star shape. Each board should have a board on top on one end and on the bottom at the other. At some point one board will have to start and finish on the same side; this is unavoidable. Work with arrangement so it lies as flat as possible. Cut four 12-inch lengths of wire and one 16-inch length to form hanging loop. Wrap wire through holes in each point a few times. Even up the length of points.

3 Drill holes at 3 intersections of the boards. Put wire through holes and wrap around boards, twisting wire at back of star.

4
GIFTS FOR GIVING

Turn to these pages when you want to give something from the heart. making a gift with your own hands just means so much more—to the recipient and to you, the creator! These gift ideas are simple to stitch, assemble or customize for friends, family or anyone else on your list. Enjoy creating—and sharing—these **Gifts for Giving.**

MEMORY/SCRAPBOOK COVER FOR THE HOLIDAYS

Create a simple holiday book cover for your picture album or scrapbook to give your favorite memories of the holidays special attention.

1 Measure the front of the book from side to side and top to bottom. Cut a scrap of linen or tea-stained background fabric slightly smaller than the cover of the album or scrapbook.

2 Using stamping ink on the holiday stamp, stamp a picture in the center of the fabric. Hand stitch the image onto the fabric using embroidery floss. (*Alternative Step 2:* Create an appliqué: Press fusible web to wrong side of a square calico scrap. On paper side of fused fabric, draw a freehand holiday shape such as a stocking or tree. Cut outline of shape, remove paper backing and fuse shape onto linen background. Blanket stitch around outline of shape. Backstitch a holiday greeting as desired.)

3 Using a rotary cutter and cutting mat, trim the linen background fabric evenly on all sides so that it fits nicely on the book cover. Fray the fabric on all four sides of the stitched piece.

4 Measure book cover from side to side on inside front, front cover, spine, back cover, and inside back **(A).** Measure book cover from top to bottom on front cover **(B)** and add ½ inch. Using a rotary cutter and mat, cut a square of decorative felt to these measurements (this example measured 39½ by 12 inches).

Book cover

Add ½" to height measurement

5 Right sides together, fold ends in, using distance measured side to side of inside front **(C)** and inside back cover **(C).** Press and pin a ⅛-inch seam allowance on top and bottom of the piece through all layers of fabric. Cut a 2- by 4-inch felt rectangle; pin to top and bottom of the open area left for spine. Using a ⅛-inch seam allowance, machine stitch. Trim, clip corners, turn right side out and press. Place cover over book.

6 Position and pin stitched piece in a pleasing position on front of the book cover. Using embroidery floss or very thin satin ribbon, attach stitched background piece to cover with a slipstitch, blanket stitch or French knots. Add your favorite pictures or scrapbooking memories to complete your holiday memories project!

BEADED ELASTIC BOOKMARK

Personalize this "stay-put" bookmark with beads and a charm for readers on your gift list. Craft stores offer a great assortment of beads and charms, so your choices are endless! For easy planning, choose a color theme or subject/hobby theme. To use the bookmark, place back cover through loop, or for paperbacks place a section through loop and use single elastic to mark your place.

MATERIALS

- Beading elastic:
- 30 inches for a small book (typical paperback size)
- 40 inches for a larger book (typical hardcover size)
- Various beads:
- At least 2 (9-mm) pony beads
- Other beads with large enough holes through which to thread elastic
- A couple small beads
- Charm (as desired)
- Size 2 crimp beads
- Headpin for alternate finish

TOOLS

- Tape measure
- Scissors
- Long-nosed pliers
- Small dish to hold beads while working

$

1 Cut beading elastic to desired length. Fold elastic back on itself at 8 inches (small) or 9½ inches (large). With overhand knot and forming a loop, knot at point where double elastic ends (leaving about a 3/4-inch tail). Add one pony bead, covering remaining elastic and tail. Loop long elastic piece back through bead and pull close to knot.

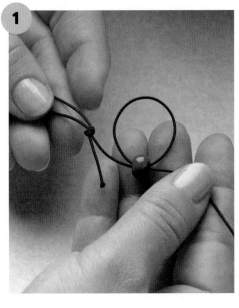

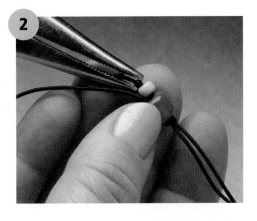

2 Add small bead to tail. Place crimp bead after small bead and squeeze crimp bead with pliers to hold in place.

3 String beads on single elastic in following order: Crimp bead, desired beads, pony bead. **Tip:** To achieve an attractive order for beads, include one larger decorative bead as focal point. Form small loop for hanging charm in the same manner as in Step 1. Let beads slide to knot. Close to top bead, squeeze crimp bead tight. Add small bead and crimp bead to tail as in Step 2. Attach charm. *Alternate finish:* String beads on headpin and form loop with pliers, place around elastic loop and close.

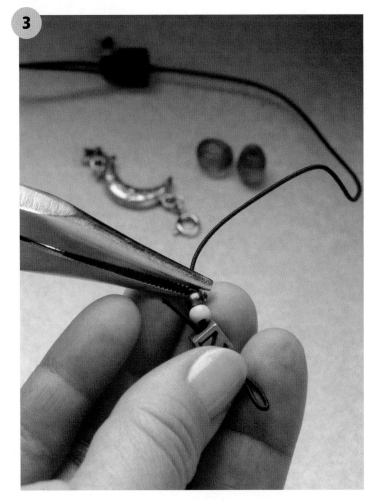

CHIC COSMETIC CASE

Create this skirt-shaped cosmetic case for someone young at heart. The key is to use a synthetic suede fabric for the outside and coordinate with a fun cotton print inside. When working with synthetic suede, do not use pins or a hot iron. Hold fabric taut as you sew.

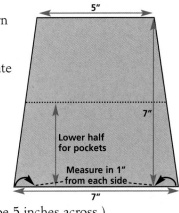

1 Enlarge pattern at right to full size (400%). Alternatively, create a pattern with a bottom line 7 inches long. For sides, measure 1 inch in from ends of bottom line and up 7 inches; connect points. (Top will be 5 inches across.)

5"

7"

Lower half for pockets

Measure in 1" from each side

7"

7"

2 Cut out pattern. From synthetic suede cut two pattern pieces. From cotton print cut two pieces larger than pattern by ½ inch at top, bottom and one side. Also cut two cotton print pieces from bottom half of pattern. From interfacing cut two pieces smaller than pattern by ¼ inch on all sides. Overlap sides of synthetic suede about ½ inch; use masking tape to hold. Stitch near edge and in a scant ⅜ inch.

3 Prepare lining: Fold ½ down and press top of pockets. Fuse with narrow strip of fusible web and place on lining. Check that interfacing fits just inside edges; stitch on outside fabric. Trim if necessary. Place interfacing on wrong side of lining, fold fabric edges and press.

4 Cut two 14-inch pieces of ribbon. Pin ribbon at center, 1 inch down from top of lining, centered. On other lining piece, place ribbon 1 inch up from pocket. Using zigzag stitch, stitch to lining. Place lining on outside pieces. Using a few small pieces of fusible, fuse with medium hot iron, to hold while stitching. Between layers, place 10-inch ribbon about 1 inch from top outside corners. Stitch around lining, near edges. Repeat.

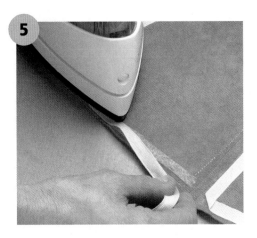

5 Position ribbon around edges on outside. Use narrow strips of fusible web to fuse ribbon in place. Take care not to iron the suede, as doing so will damage the fabric. Iron only on the ribbon.

COOKIES-IN-A-JAR

An eye-catching, mouth-watering gift that is inexpensive to make and yields delicious results.

MATERIALS

- 1-quart canning jar with lid/cover
- Recipe ingredients (in shaded boxes at right)
- Fabric scrap to cover lid
- 1 yard of ribbon
- Paper for making instruction sheet
- Decorative paper

TOOLS

- Measuring cups
- Measuring spoons

$

This is a perfect "handmade" gift to give because who doesn't love to eat cookies! **1** Use the freshest ingredients, and the gift will have a shelf life of about 3 months. The ingredients can be layered, giving the appearance of sand art, or you can shake them up for an all-over appearance. **2** If you are layering, put flour/baking powder/salt on the bottom level, sugars next, nuts and candies on the top. **3** To make it really special, cut out a 9-inch circle of fabric to cover the jar with, and tie it on with some ribbon. Complete the gift with handwritten or computer-printed directions. The recipient will have to add fresh ingredients (eggs, butter, vanilla). This idea can be used for all of your favorite cookie recipes, as long as they fit in a 1-quart jar.

M & M COOKIES-IN-A-JAR RECIPE

1 *To fill the jar:* In a bowl, combine the flour with the baking soda, salt, and sugar. This makes the "white" layer. Spoon this into the canning jar. On top of that, put in the brown sugar. Use a big spoon to tamp it down as evenly as possible. Lastly, pour in the M & M Mini Baking Bits.

2 cups all-purpose flour
1/2 teaspoon baking soda
1/4 teaspoon salt
1/4 cup white sugar
3/4 cup packed brown sugar
1 1/2 cups M & M Mini Baking Bits

2 Attach a card with the following directions:
M & M COOKIES-IN-A-JAR
Preheat oven to 350°F. Into large mixing bowl, empty jar contents and mix until all ingredients are well combined. Using your hands work in **3/4 cup softened butter or margarine.** In separate bowl, beat **1 egg** with **1 teaspoon vanilla extract.** Work egg mixture into jar contents mixture until well combined. Shape dough into 1-inch-sized balls and place on ungreased baking sheet or baking sheet with parchment paper 2 inches apart. Slightly flatten the balls with the palm of your hand. Bake 10 to 14 minutes or until edges are lightly browned. Remove cookies to a rack to cool. Makes about 2 dozen cookies.

OATMEAL CHERRY COOKIES-IN-A-JAR RECIPE

1 *To fill the jar:* Combine flour, baking soda, salt and sugar together in a bowl. Mix thoroughly and pour into jar. Add oats. On top of that, add brown sugar and tamp down with a large spoon. Lastly, pour in dried cherries.

3/4 cup flour
1/2 teaspoon baking soda
1/4 teaspoon salt
1/4 cup sugar
1 1/2 cups quick or old fashioned oats
1/2 cup firmly packed brown sugar
1/2 cup dried cherries

2 Attach a card with the following directions:
OATMEAL CHERRY COOKIES-IN-A-JAR
Preheat oven to 350°F. Into large mixing bowl, empty jar contents and mix until all ingredients are well combined. Using your hands work in **1 stick softened butter or margarine.** In separate bowl, beat **1 egg** with **1/2 teaspoon vanilla extract.** Work egg mixture into jar contents mixture until well combined. Drop by rounded tablespoonfuls onto ungreased cookie sheet. Bake 10 to 12 minutes or until golden brown. Cool 1 minute on cookie sheet. Remove to wire rack. Makes about 2 dozen cookies.

BROWNIE MIX IN-A-JAR RECIPE

1 *To fill the jar:* Layer ingredients in order listed, packing down firmly after each addition.

1 1/2 cups flour
1/3 cup unsweetened cocoa powder
1/3 cup flaked coconut
1/2 cup semisweet chocolate chips
3/4 cup white sugar
1/3 cup chopped pecans
2/3 cup packed brown sugar

2 Attach a card with the following directions:
BROWNIES-IN-A-JAR
Preheat oven to 350°F. Grease an 8- by 8-inch square pan. In a large bowl, stir together **2 eggs, 2/3 cup oil** and **1 teaspoon vanilla.** Stir in jar contents; mix well. Spread mixture evenly into prepared pan. Bake 25 to 30 minutes or until toothpick inserted into brownies comes out clean. Allow to cool. Cut into squares. Makes 16 brownies.

HOLIDAY HAND-STAMPED PICTURE FRAME

Every snowflake brings to mind how special you are - you're one of a kind!

Frame a special photo in this simply created picture frame. A custom-framed photo makes a perfect gift for friends or family.

- 1 8½- x 11-inch piece of card stock in each of the following colors:
  - White
  - Navy blue
  - Green
  - Red
- Special family photos
- Double-sided tape or tabs
- Color-coordinated stamping ink pad

TOOLS

- Rotary cutter and cutting mat (or other paper cutter)
- Scissors
- Snowflake punch
- Holiday stamp(s)
- Decorative corner punch or scissors
- Circle or oval cutter
- Razor blade or craft knife

$$$

1 Cut white and navy blue card stock each into four 4¼- by 5½-inch card pieces. (One or more of these will be used for the project. Use the extra pieces to practice on.) From red card stock, cut one 4½- by 5¾-inch card piece. From green card stock, cut two card pieces each 4¾ by 6 inches. With a decorative paper punch, trim all corners on all card pieces.

2 Using a circle cutter and mat, cut a small (2-inch-diameter) hole at the left side of one white card piece. Using color-coordinated stamping ink, stamp a holiday stamp on the right side of the card piece. Use the snowflake punch to punch a few snowflakes on the card, being careful not to punch the hole or the stamped area.

3 Position photo in the hole area; attach using double-stick tape. Trim picture so edges do not show through punched snowflakes. Position decorated white card piece over blue card piece; attach with double-stick tape. Make sure blue shows only through punched snowflakes and not around white edges.

4 Position the assembled white and blue card piece in center of red card piece, leaving ⅛-inch red edge showing. Attach to red piece with double-stick tape. Position layered card in center of green card piece, leaving ⅛-inch green edge showing. Attach to green piece with double-stick tape. With razor blade, cut a necktie-shaped wedge out of remaining green card piece. Bend wedge out to allow card to sit up like a picture frame. With double-stick tape, attach green wedge to back of assembled cards. **Finishing tips:** Slip framed photo into an envelope with a special expression of giving noted in handwritten calligraphy or a computer-generated font. Cut a few blue snowflakes from the blue scraps of card stock and attach to the envelope. Give the frame and picture as a special gift.

LAVENDER-SCENTED EYE PILLOW

This soothing and relaxing, lavender-scented eye pillow is the perfect spa gift for everyone on your gift-giving list!

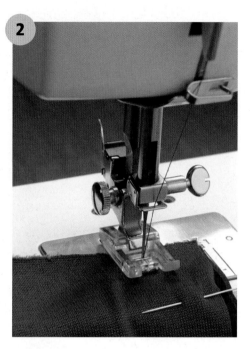

1 Place a business-size paper envelope (4⅛ by 9½ inches) onto velour; pin securely in place. Using envelope as a template, cut out fabric. Repeat procedure with satin fabric.

2 Right sides facing, sew along both long sides and one short side of the fabric, leaving one short side unfinished. Turn fabric inside out.

3 Fill eye pillow with rice and dried lavender. (Scented dried lavender can be purchased in the section of the store near the candles.) Turn about ¼ inch of unsewn edges toward inside. With a whipstitch, hand sew edge securely to enclose rice and lavender.

4 The eye pillow can be heated in the microwave for 30 to 40 seconds on high to become a soothing treat for tired eyes. For gift giving, create a spa package in a decorative box or wicker basket. Along with the eye pillow (and heating instructions), include assorted lotions, foaming bath gels, bath confetti and massagers.

113

CHRISTMAS CLUTCH BAG

Make this elegant holiday purse for
a gift or for yourself. It is quick and
easy and made from a placemat.

MATERIALS

- 2 (13- by 18-inch) placemats
- 3 (¾-inch) magnets
- 3 (¾-inch) washers
- 4 popsicle sticks
- Matching thread
- Beads (optional)

TOOLS

- Marking pencil
- See-through ruler
- Shears
- Sewing machine and zipper foot
- Paper and pencil for pattern

$

1 Fold 1¼-inch casing on a short end of placemat. Place one magnet centered and one on each end ¾ inch from the edge. Between magnets, place a popsicle stick. Stitch casing along edge using zipper foot. On opposite short side, fold casing 1¼ inches. Place washers, centered and ¾ inch from each end. Stitch around each washer to hold in place. Place sticks between washers; stitch casing along edge.

2 On other placemat, mark a 13-inch square. Mark diagonal (AB) and cut. Zigzag stitch or serge the diagonal edge. Fold points A and B in 1½ inches and press. Position diagonal on right side of placemat just covering casing stitching line; pin. Stitch flap in place.

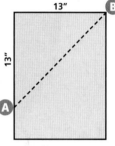

3 Create paper gusset (side) pattern by marking 2 parallel lines 5 inches long and 3 inches apart. Mark half circle at one end. Cut. Place the short straight edge along finished edge of placemat. Mark and cut. Cut a second gusset. Mark center of curved end and center of long side of placemat. Pin right sides together at marks. With gusset facing up, stitch, using a ¼-inch seam allowance and pulling curve to match straight side as stitching. Starting from center, stitch other side of gusset. Repeat for other end. Turn to right side and tuck gusset top to inside. The placemat in this example had beads on each corner; however, if mat does not have beads, add beads to flap to add weight.

COFFEE LOVERS' DREAM

Vanilla Sugar

Cocoa Pow

Chocolate

Holiday Coffee Mocha
Serves 6

*The perfect gift for coffee lovers on your list!
Homemade vanilla sugar, chocolate shavings,
cocoa and a tasty, yet simple coffee house
style recipe for mochas complete this package.*

1 Place the sugar in a large bowl. Using a knife, split vanilla beans lengthwise. Scrape seeds from bean center into bowl with sugar; add vanilla bean shells to sugar mixture. Stir to mix vanilla seeds evenly into sugar. Cover bowl with plastic wrap or place sugar mixture in airtight container. Allow to sit for one to two weeks to infuse the sugar with vanilla. Place sugar in small decorative glass jars.

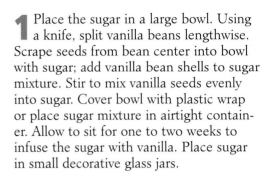

2 Using vegetable peeler, "peel" chocolate bars to create chocolate shavings. Place shavings in decorative glass jar. Place cocoa powder in separate decorative glass jar.

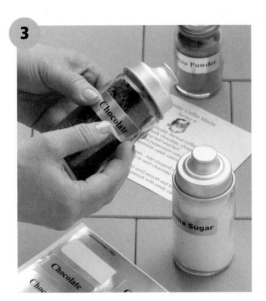

3 Make jar labels from decorative silver mailing labels (purchased at office supply stores). Print jar contents, such as "vanilla sugar" or "chocolate shavings" and affix to each jar.

4 On a computer or by hand, print recipe cards for Holiday Coffee Mochas using the following recipe. For gift giving, place recipe card and assorted glass jars into small basket or decorative box along with a coffee mug.

HOLIDAY COFFEE MOCHAS

1 Pour coffee into large saucepan. Add chocolate; cook on low heat 4 to 6 minutes or until chocolate is melted.

2 Add half-and-half and extract; stir until smooth and blended. Pour into coffee mugs and garnish with candy canes.

- 5 cups freshly brewed coffee
- 4 ounces milk chocolate, chopped
- 1 cup half-and-half
- 1 teaspoon peppermint extract
- 6 peppermint candy canes

FABRIC BUSINESS CARD CARRIER

Using a sturdy rich-looking fabric, trim and an antique or unique button, make this one-of-a-kind business or credit card carrier. With minimal machine sewing, it is easy to make and looks very elegant. Spray with a fabric protectant before using.

MATERIALS

- 5½- by 8-inch scrap of sturdy decorative fabric
- 8- by 5-inch scrap of medium-weight cotton woven fabric (like quilting fabric)
- 4- by 12-inch piece of fusible interfacing
- 5½-inch length (1- or 1½-inch wide) lace
- 1-inch decorative button
- Smaller plain button
- Matching or metallic thread
- 12 inches of decorative ribbon or cording

TOOLS

- Shears or rotary cutter and cutting mat
- See-through ruler
- Pins
- Iron

1 Cut fabric: From interfacing cut one 4- by 5-inch piece and one 4- by 7-inch piece. From cotton, cut one piece 8 by 5 inches. From decorative fabric cut one piece 5½ by 8 inches. Center 4- by 5-inch interfacing piece on cotton piece with 2 inches of fabric showing on each side; fuse. Center 4- by 7-inch piece of interfacing on decorative fabric with about ½ inch of fabric showing on all sides. Fuse.

2 To assemble inside divider, fold the 2 inches of fabric on each side toward center; press. Fold in half crosswise; press. Position lace near fold; pin. Using matching thread, stitch each side near edge.

3 To assemble outside, fold long sides in ½ inch; press. Check width against inside divider to ensure accuracy. Mark 3 inches from bottom and fold to mark; press. Fold top down almost to that mark; press. Fold bottom to top at 3-inch mark. Mark center placement for decorative button. For smaller button, mark top back center placement. Sew buttons with matching thread. To finish, place divider inside folded decorative fabric and align ends. Use blanket or zigzag stitch to stitch sides. Reinforce corners of outside pocket using very short, wide zigzag stitch. Tie cording around back button.

LET IT SNOW BEADED PICTURE FRAME

Turn a plain picture frame into a winter wonderland in no time. All it takes is colored beads and a little imagination!

1 Clean frame and glass thoroughly to remove smudges and ensure that glue and beads will stick well. On outermost crevice of frame, just inside outer edge, make single-color beaded border (blue in sample): Apply glue line two to three inches long and, using tweezers, place beads on glue. Continue making short lines with glue and placing beads to complete entire border. **Tip:** Larger beads work best for border.

2 At top of frame on border, draw each letter separately with glue for the words "LET IT SNOW". Using single-color bead, place beads onto glue-written words. **Tip:** Draw words letter by letter to avoid the glue drying before beads are in place.

3 On glass portion of frame, draw snowflakes with glue; top with silver- and white-colored beads. Rectangular beads and round beads work best to create the snowflake shapes. If desired, purchase beaded snowflake shapes at a craft or hobby store instead of creating your own. Scatter assorted color beads around snowflakes to create a "snow" effect.

5
GIFT WRAPPING

Whether you've made a gift by hand or carefully selected one from a store or catalog, you'll love showing your creativity with these artful cards, tags and wrap. There is an art to giving presents, and **Gift Wrapping** has never been so fun and satisfying!

FUN AND FUNKY GIFT TAGS

"Capture" some fun and insert it into a funky gift tag that looks cute and moves when you shake it.

MATERIALS

- Extra wrapping paper or old holiday cards (or color-copied photos of family members sitting on Santa's lap when they were little)
- Glue or glue stick
- Card stock paper or decorative scrapbooking paper
- Small items to fill gift tag with, such as metallic stars, candy canes, snowflakes
- ¼ yard clear vinyl (found in fabric store)
- 3 silver pipe cleaners

TOOLS

- Scissors
- Scrapbooking scissors with deckle edge (optional)
- Hot glue gun and glue sticks
- Sewing machine
- Hole punch

$

1 From wrapping paper, cut out an image using scrapbooking scissors. Glue image onto colored card stock paper (or decorative scrapbooking paper). To frame image, cut away all but about ¼ inch of card stock paper. Write your "TO" and "FROM" message on back of card stock.

2 Position assembled image piece onto vinyl. Fold excess vinyl up and over top of image. Cut vinyl around image piece, leaving about 1 inch of vinyl around sides and top, and about ¼ inch at bottom fold. Open vinyl. With glue gun, run line of hot glue around back edges of image piece; lay it in place on vinyl.

3 Fold vinyl up over image piece; image will be encased in vinyl with about 1 inch of vinyl around three edges. Sew vinyl packet along both side edges, about ¼ inch from each edge. (Do not sew bottom fold or top edge.)

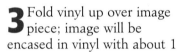

4 In upper right-hand corner of vinyl packet, use hole punch to punch 1 hole through vinyl and image piece. Fill vinyl packet with trinkets. Sew top of vinyl packet closed, about ¼ inch from edge of image piece. Trim vinyl very close to stitching.

5 Over stitching lines and along bottom edge of packet, run a line of hot glue onto which you will affix pipe cleaner. **Tip:** Apply glue to only one edge at a time and let glue cool before proceeding. Fold one silver pipe cleaner in half, forming a loop; push it through punched hole. Pull pipe cleaner ends through loop, and tighten to form bendable tail. In upper left-hand corner on pipe cleaner border, hot-glue artificial leaves and berries to finish up.

SEASONS GREETINGS FOLD-OUT CARD

This holiday greeting stands out because it's a stand-up, folding card. Creating a one-of-a-kind greeting card is as simple as writing, cutting, folding and adding a holiday family photo.

MATERIALS

- 1 (3½- by 1½-inch) piece standard paper
- 2 (5½- by 8½-inch) pieces medium-weight paper, each the same color or in contrasting colors
- Invisible tape
- Holiday photograph
- 1 (5½- by 4½-inch) envelope

TOOLS

- Pencil
- Glue stick
- Craft knife
- Folding stick (or wooden popsicle stick)

$

1 Decide on a one- or two-word greeting to write on your card's fold-out. On 3½- by 1½-inch piece of standard paper, print greeting by hand or using an ink jet printer. Place printed greeting onto one 5½- by 8½-inch piece medium-weight paper to use as a pattern. Position onto center of sheet, centering greeting. Tape in place on top and bottom edges.

2 Using craft knife, cut vertical lines through medium-weight paper to mark beginning and ending of greeting pattern. Cutting through greeting pattern just onto surface of medium-weight paper, cut letters out, leaving space around letters uncut. (Cuts will score medium paper surface.)

3 Remove greeting pattern. On scored letters, make clean cuts through medium-weight paper until letters are clearly cut.

4 Fold cut medium-weight paper in half. Fold greeting design toward you. Use folding stick to mark top edge of fold. Open folded paper; greeting design pushes outward. Fold paper in half again, gently pushing to keep greeting design inside. Use folding stick to score top and bottom edges of greeting design. Now as you open the card, the word design will pop out as a fold-out design.

5 Fold other piece of medium-weight paper in half. Use glue stick to glue fold-out card to second medium-weight folded piece. Choose holiday photo to place above fold-out. Write message on lower part of card. Add decorations to envelope and send off your one-of-a-kind, fold-out greeting card to a friend or family member.

HOLIDAY GIFT TAGS

Decorate your gifts for the holiday season with chalkboard wood shapes. Address tags with chalk, erase later and reuse for next season's gift giving.

MATERIALS

- Wood holiday shapes (available at craft stores)
- 1 wet paper towel
- Old newspaper
- Spray acrylic paint primer
- Spray chalkboard paint
- Colorful ribbons

TOOLS

- Chalk
- Pencil
- Hand drill
- Scissors
- 1- by 1-inch piece of fine-grain sandpaper

1 On each wood shape, use a pencil to mark position of hole for tag. Drill hole from one side of shape; turn over and drill through other side of shape. (This prevents wood from splintering around hole.) Roll ends of small sandpaper square over to fit inside drilled hole. Sand gently to remove rough edges. Unroll sandpaper and sand any rough surface areas on front and back of each shape. Use wet paper towel to clean remaining sawdust off each shape; allow to dry.

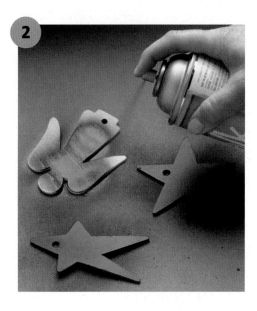

2 Arrange wooden shapes on old newspaper with 2 inches between each shape. Working in a well-ventilated location, spray each side of wooden shape with acrylic paint primer. (Shake acrylic paint primer paint can before use, and spray each side of wooden shapes with a sweeping motion, 10 inches from surface.) Allow to dry and repeat on other side.

3 Once shapes have dried completely, repeat spray-painting process with chalkboard paint. Apply paint in thin coats to avoid drips. For best results use two coats of chalkboard spray.

4 Wait 24 hours before marking on chalkboard surface. Prepare surface by rubbing chalk over entire surface area and erasing. (Use calcium carbonate chalk for best results.) Select colorful ribbons to cut for tags. Use scissors to cut to desired length. Cut ribbon ends at a diagonal, or make a V cut by folding ribbon ends together and cutting diagonally. Thread ribbon through tag hole and pull halfway through hole. Fan ribbon out to reshape into a bow, or simply tie off and let ribbon ends hang loose. Use chalk to address your holiday tag. Erase with felt eraser. Reuse tags by changing names and ribbons.

FRIENDLY
FELLAS
WRAP
AND
TAGS

The kids will love potato-stamping designs that turn
ordinary kraft paper into playful wrap and gift tags.

MATERIALS

• Kraft paper
• Potatoes
• White acrylic paint
• Silver glitter, optional
• Color card stock
• Cord and ribbon

TOOLS

• Paring knife
• Small flat paintbrush
• Marking pens in black and other desired colors
• Pencil with eraser
• Scissors
• Paper punch
• Glue stick

1 Cut the desired size of kraft paper. If you choose, you could wrap the gift before painting the paper.

2 On protected work surface, cut two or three potatoes in half, cutting some lengthwise to make various shapes and sizes of stamps.

3 To stamp a snowman, use two sizes of potato stamps. For snowman body, brush paint on flat area of larger potato; stamp on paper as shown in photo. For snowman head, brush paint on flat area of smaller potato; stamp above body. If desired, use

paintbrush to smooth out stamped paint. Continue stamping snowmen randomly, or in a pattern, until desired look is achieved. To make paper "ribbon," stamp designs on kraft paper strip. Let stamped paper dry.

4 As shown in photo, use marking pens to draw hats, scarves, arms and faces on snowmen.

5 To add large snowflakes, dip pencil eraser in paint and dot onto surface. Sprinkle with glitter if desired. For small snowflakes, dip paintbrush handle into paint and dot onto surface; let dry.

6 To make tags, cut out a single stamped snowman. Glue to card stock allowing space for writing at bottom; trim. Punch hole at top and insert cord.

PURSE-SHAPED GIFT BAG

Using heavy decorative paper, create this gift bag to resemble a purse. It is cute and feminine for a small gift for a special girl or lady. Use her favorite colors or traditional Christmas colors. Stuff colorful tissue paper to the top.

MATERIALS

- 19- by 15-inch piece of heavy decorative paper or card stock
- Brown paper bag, opened up flat
- Double-stick tape
- 18 inches (1/4-inch) trim
- 16 inches bead trim
- Decorative yarn or feather trim

TOOLS

- See-through ruler or plastic T square
- Sharp pencil
- Scissors

$

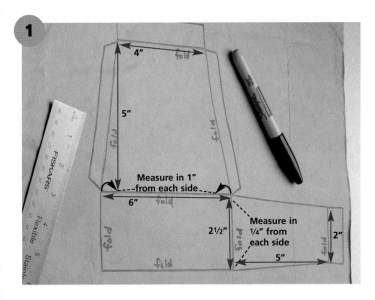

1 Starting in center of flat paper bag, draw one 6- by 2½-inch rectangle. (This will be purse bottom.) On each long edge of rectangle, measure 1 inch in from corner and 5 inches up; mark. On each side, connect rectangle corner to 5-inch mark with diagonal line; connect ends of each diagonal line. On each side, draw parallel line ½ inch to outside of diagonal line. Connect ends of parallel lines with angled lines. Draw parallel line ¾ inch above top line. (These diagonal-sided pieces will be the front and back of purse.) From each short end of rectangle, measure ¼ inch in from corner and 5 inches up; mark. On each short side, connect rectangle corner to 5-inch mark with diagonal line. Draw parallel line ¾ inch outside "top" line. (These narrow pieces will be the purse sides.)

2 Cut out pattern and trace onto right side of decorative paper. Gently fold bottom rectangle along line. Fold sides up at fold line. On front and back pieces, fold ½-inch extensions in. Place double-stick tape along side edges on inside of purse, working on one side of purse at a time. Bring each side together with front and back. **Tip:** Use eraser end of pencil to get inside to affix tape. Fold top extensions down inside and hold in place with tape.

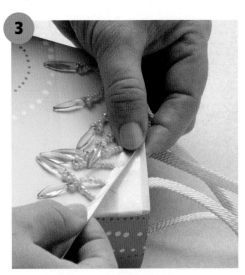

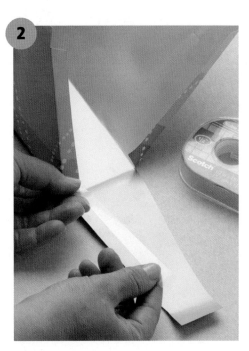

3 Cut two 8- to 10-inch pieces of trim. **Tip:** Tape ends before cutting. Tape ends inside, about 1 inch from sides. Starting at one side, place bead trim around top of purse; use tape to hold in place. Wrap decorative yarn or other trim over bead trim ribbon, using tape to hold in place.

PLAYFUL POP-UP CARDS

A few cuts on paper and dabs of glue are all it takes to make jolly cards with personality that pops.

MATERIALS

- 2 (12-inch) squares of coordinating patterned scrapbook papers
- Tracing paper
- 8½- by 11-inch white card stock
- Scrap of orange paper
- Scrap of contrasting paper for scarf and hat brim
- Business-size envelopes

TOOLS

- Ruler
- Pencil
- Scissors
- Glue stick
- Black fine-tip marking pen

1 On each square of patterned scrapbook paper, cut one 9- by 7¾-inch rectangle.

2 Fold rectangle for card front in half, long ends and wrong sides together.

3 Fold rectangle for card inside in half, long ends and right sides together. With fold at top, mark on the fold 2 inches from left corner. Repeat, 2 inches from right corner. Using marks as guides, cut two 1½-inch slits perpendicular to fold, as shown in photo 3. Fold down tab as shown in Photo 3B. Open card; pop out tab.

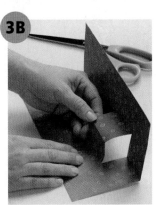

4 Enlarge pattern pieces by 200%. Use patterns to trace snowman face and body on white card stock, nose on orange paper, and scarf and hatband on a contrasting paper scrap. Cut out each traced piece. From leftover card front paper, cut hat brim and one 2¼- by 3-inch rectangle for hat. Fold hat rectangle in half, short ends and wrong sides together.

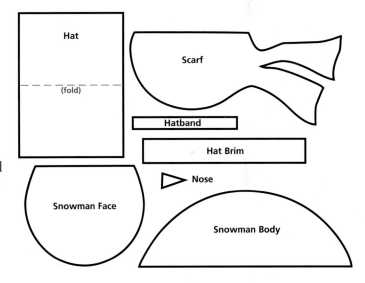

Hat

(fold)

Scarf

Hatband

Hat Brim

Nose

Snowman Face

Snowman Body

5 For the message areas, cut rectangles from white paper, backing with contrasting paper. Glue shapes to card, starting with snowman body centered under tab as shown in photo. Glue message rectangles to card. Glue down scarf, head, hat pieces and nose. Adhere the two card layers together; do not glue pop-up tab. Draw in face details and write in messages.

6 Embellish envelope flaps with desired paper shapes. Address the envelope and drop in the mail!

6
FESTIVE TABLE

Opportunities for celebrations and entertaining fill the holiday season. Make your table memorable with unique and creative accessories like the ones here—Candy "Cracker" place cards, customized napkin rings, beautiful table linens and much more. Creating a **Festive Table** is fun, easy and rewarding.

CANDY "CRACKER" PLACE CARDS

Based on the ever-popular Christmas Crackers, this craft doubles as an attractive embellishment to adorn your table and a candy- and greeting-filled place card for guests.

MATERIALS

- Wrapping paper
- Toilet paper rolls
- 2-inch-wide decorative ribbon
- Clear cellophane
- Clear tape
- Small candies
- Fortunes or greetings
- Curling ribbon
- Large star-shaped gift tags

TOOLS

- Scissors
- Glue stick

$

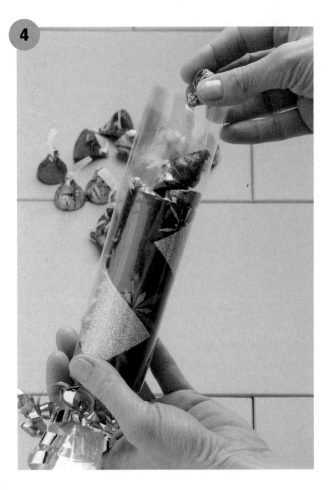

1 Cut a piece of wrapping paper 4½ inches wide by 12 inches long. Using glue stick, cover back surface of wrapping paper with glue. Cover toilet paper roll with wrapping paper, being careful to roll up tightly so paper covers the surface flat and without bumps.

2 Cut 5-inch-long piece of decorative ribbon. Using glue stick, cover back surface of ribbon with glue. Starting at one end of covered toilet paper roll, glue ribbon diagonally around roll, finishing at opposite end.

3 Cut a piece of clear cellophane 12 inches wide by 16 inches long. Cover toilet paper roll in cellophane by rolling it up. Using clear tape, secure cellophane by taping in place in center of roll.

4 Fill "cracker" with small pieces of candy. To each "cracker," add small fortune-sized piece of paper with Christmas greeting or fortune for the coming year. (These can be handwritten or printed on the computer and then cut out.) With curling ribbon, secure "cracker" ends by tying ribbon around each end. Write each guest's name on star-shaped gift tag; secure tags by tying onto curling ribbon at one end of "cracker."

CHRISTMAS CANDY TREE

This magical craft is both functional and beautiful, adorned with candy and embellished with garlands of curling ribbon and "bulbs" of mini bows.

MATERIALS

- 12- by 3-inch styrofoam shaped cone
- Aluminum foil
- Assorted wrapped candies (for example, mini candy bars, peppermint candies and mini chocolate cone shaped candy)
- Curling ribbon or curl swirled bows
- Mini bows

TOOLS

- Hot glue gun and glue sticks

$$

1 Cover entire styrofoam cone with aluminum foil. Secure foil using hot glue gun.

2 Prepare to hot-glue candies to tree. (Read Step 2 completely before continuing. Plan to place largest pieces of candy near bottom of tree. (This helps create Christmas tree shape and also helps stabilize tree.) For candies such as mini candy bars and peppermint candies, apply glue only to one edge of foil or plastic wrapper. For candies such as mini chocolate cone shaped candy, glue flat side directly to foil.

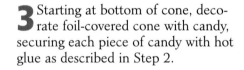

3 Starting at bottom of cone, decorate foil-covered cone with candy, securing each piece of candy with hot glue as described in Step 2.

4 Glue strips of curling ribbon or pieces of curl swirled bows to tree to look like garland. (Curl swirled bows can be easily taken apart into strips perfect for decorating tree; simply remove staple that secures curled ribbon strands.) For tree topper, hot-glue mini bow to top of tree. If desired, glue additional mini bows onto candy covered tree to look like bulbs.

JINGLE BELL NAPKIN RING

Create a festive look for your holiday table with this napkin ring made from jingle bells. You can find bells in a variety of colors, and you can even purchase wire in traditional Christmas colors if you want.

1 Cut a 12-inch piece of wire. String jingle bells in alternating colors, shaking them together so they overlap. One 12-inch piece of wire requires about 39 bells, but check size by holding wire together and creating a circle. The inner circle should be at least 1½ inches (or hold work-in-progress around cloth napkin to check).

2 Pull wire ends together and close to end bells. Using pliers, twist wire a few times. **Tip:** Insert napkin in napkin ring to hold it up while completing the project.

3 Hang one bell from each wire end; using pliers, twist wire back on itself. (Wire ends do not need to be equal.) Hot-glue an embellishment near base of wires.

GOLD STAR PLACEMAT

It is easy to create a 5-point star, using a continuous length of ribbon. Choose woven ribbon (not craft ribbon) that is similar on both front and back. Satin or grosgrain ribbon works well.

MATERIALS

- Purchased placemat in coordinating color and fabric
- 2½ yards (⅞-inch) woven ribbon
- 2-yards (¾-inch-wide roll) fusible web strips
- Matching fine machine embroidery thread

TOOLS

- Straight pins
- Iron
- Sewing machine and new size 11 needle

$

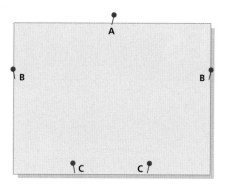

1 On purchased placemat, mark the following points with pins: Top center **(A)**; on each side, 4 inches down from top **(B)**; along bottom edge, 5 inches in from each side **(C)**. With fusible web strips, connect marks to form star shape; pin fusible web in place.

2 Steam-shrink ribbon by ironing with medium-plus-steam setting.

3 Use ironing board as work surface. Starting in lower right corner, place ribbon from there to top center. (Let 1 inch overlap placemat at starting point.) Using medium iron setting, fuse ribbon to placemat, taking care not to touch iron to exposed fusible web. At top point, fold ribbon, following fusible web line; press tip gently after removing pin. Continue around star-shape. After fusible web is covered, gently press (do not move iron while on ribbon). At end, fold ribbon under starting point in the same direction as starting point. Trim ribbon.

4 With a narrow, medium-length zigzag stitch, stitch close to each edge of ribbon. Stitch each edge in the same direction. While stitching, hold fabric taut in front of and behind stitching area. To secure beginning and end of stitching, pull top thread to back and knot threads together.

TULLE TREES

Group these delicate, airy trees in various sizes on a mantel or buffet. Using tulle, purchased by the roll, and small Christmas balls, the combinations are endless. Trees can vary in size from 4 inches to 10 inches, so choose proportionately sized balls.

1 Cut tulle into 3- by 3-inch squares. For a fuller look, crisscross two pieces of tulle. (For 4-inch cone, you may want to cut tulle pieces smaller, such as 2½ by 2½ inches square.)

2 Center tulle squares at desired location; using chopstick, poke into styrofoam cone. Alternate with Christmas ball (Step 3). **Tip:** When creating tree from smallest cone, first apply all the Christmas balls, then apply tulle squares. For an airy look that almost covers the balls, leave finished small tree as is. For a more polished look, trim some tulle on smaller tree away.

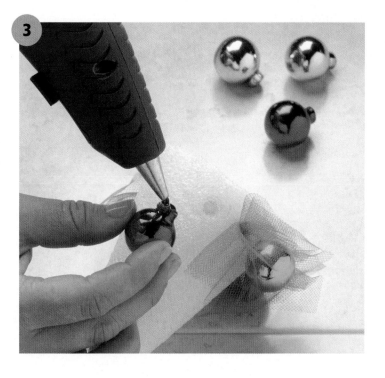

3 To attach Christmas balls, remove hanger from top of ball. Create indentation in tree by pushing ball into styrofoam cone and removing. Place a dot of hot glue on indentation. Position ball and push into cone. Alternate until reaching top. In same indentation—glue manner, place ball on top. Tie some garland around top.

ELEGANT RIBBON NAPKIN RING

This easy-to-make napkin ring requires only a little sewing. Choose from a wide variety of ribbons, including satin, woven or wire-edged. Embellish with any elegant holiday silk blossom or floral pick.

MATERIALS

- 2½-inch-wide ribbon
- ⅜-inch-wide elastic
- Matching thread
- Poinsettia blossom or holiday floral pick (embellishment)

TOOLS

- Shears
- Pins
- Sewing machine
- Glue gun and glue sticks

$

1 Measure 24 inches of ribbon; cut, then fold in half. Starting at folded end, center 15-inch length of elastic between ribbon halves; pin. Stitch through ribbon and elastic near folded edge, using very short zigzag stitch. Stitch ⅝-inch casing, centered and along length of ribbon. Do not catch elastic. (Photo illustrates stitching with contrasting thread.)

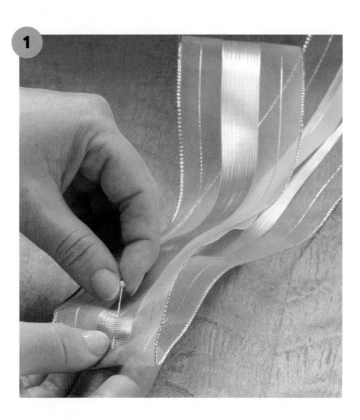

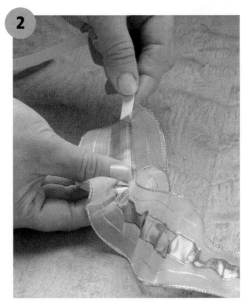

2 To gather ribbon, pull tail of elastic until gathered ribbon measures about 6 inches. To hold in place, zigzag over elastic and ribbon as above. Cut off extra elastic. Zigzag raw edges of ribbon using medium-length zigzag stitch.

3 With gathered ribbon, form circle, overlapping about ½ inch and keeping folded edge on top. Pin. Stitch at center of overlap using a very short, wide zigzag stitch.

4 Put napkin in ring to make finishing easier. Hot-glue embellishment to side of napkin ring, covering overlap. Let dry.

FESTIVE LIGHTING

Set the mood with this
easy and elegant toast
of light. Illuminate your
holiday table with tea
lights, wine glasses and
a cutout shade.

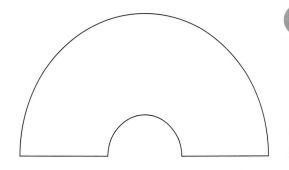

1 Enlarge shade pattern by 400%. Place vellum sheet over enlarged pattern. Use pencil to trace pattern onto vellum sheet. Cut shade shape from vellum. For multiple shades, retrace design and cut each individually.

2 Use craft punch to design a pattern of open light across shade. Starting at lower edge, punch snowflakes, making sure not to cut through edge. Leave ¼ inch on vertical edges. Next start at the top of shade, punching snowflakes without cutting over edge. If desired, save snowflake cutouts for Step 3. Bring vertical edges together; glue with glue stick and hold to make solid contact.

3 Place tea light into wine glass. Place shade over glass and set on table. Collect snowflake cutouts and scatter them on table at base of wine stem. Light candle and enjoy the glow of this festive light. (Do not leave candles unattended.)

WREATH CENTERPIECE OR ADVENT WREATH

Brighten your table with a centerpiece made from a wire wreath form, garland, candles and special embellishments.

- 12-inch wire wreath form
- 1¼-inch wood candle cups
- Candles
- 6-foot evergreen garland with shorter needles
- Green twist ties or florist wire
- 4 floral picks or bows

TOOLS

- Masking tape
- Glue gun and glue sticks
- Pliers/wire cutters

$

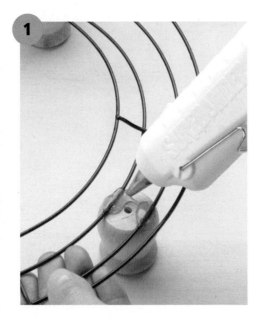

1 Divide wreath form evenly in quarters; mark with tape. Place candle cups upside down on work surface. Place wreath upside down on top of candle cups. Arrange so candle cups are at quarter marks. Using glue gun, apply liberal amount of glue to bottom of one candle cup and position wreath form on cup. Add more glue, covering the wire. Let set a moment. Repeat for each candle cup.

2 With twist tie, attach one end of garland to outside wire of wreath form. From wrong side, continue wrapping garland; as you go, attach to wire with twist ties. As you work, position evergreen ends toward front of wreath. When outside ring is complete, attach garland with twist tie. Twist garland from front to inside wire of wreath form. From back, attach garland with twist tie. Position garland around inside wire, bending slightly around candle cups and attaching as you go. If you have extra garland at the end, cut it off.

3 Arrange evergreen ends to cover wire. Between each candle cup, position flower pick or bow. Attach through to back; wrap wire stem around wire of wreath form. If using bow, attach with twist tie or floral wire through to back of wreath form.

Tip: To make this wreath for Advent, use pink and purple bows between candles and use 3 purple candles and 1 pink candle.

GATHERED HOLIDAY TABLECLOTH

Bring holiday brightness to your card table, dining table or accent table by making a fabric cover that is custom fit. If possible, purchase 60-inch-wide fabric to avoid having a seam. Add your own embellishments that can be removed or changed, as desired.

MATERIALS

- 1¾ yards (60- by 60-inch) holiday fabric
- 2 yards (⅞-inch-wide) matching single-fold bias tape
- 4 yards matching rattail cording (or similar cording)
- Matching thread
- Embellishments such as wire ribbon, pinecones or floral picks

TOOLS

- Shears
- Straight pins
- 5 large safety pins
- Iron
- Sewing machine
- Hand sewing needle

$$

1 Directions are for covering a typical card table and using a 60-inch square of fabric. To adapt, measure table and figure about an 18-inch drop on all sides. Square up fabric by folding it in half and in half the opposite direction. Line up edges and corners. Trim uneven edges. Cut corners on diagonal while fabric is folded: Measure 3 inches up from corner on both sides, mark diagonal and cut. Place on table, positioning fabric so that equal lengths drape on each side. Pin at each table corner.

2 Remove cloth to work surface. Check each corner to see that pin is on true diagonal by folding fabric on diagonal. Pin at 17 inches from corner. Position bias tape, centered at corner; fold under ½ inch and pin. Run bias to pin at 17-inch point, turn under ½ inch and pin. Pin along bias. Repeat for each corner.

3 Stitch each side of bias near edge. Take care not to stretch fabric as you sew. Stitch in the same direction for both bias edges. Fold 36-inch cording in half; place one large safety pin at fold. Using pin, thread cording through casing, starting at corner.

4 Stitch top, center end of casing, using very short zigzag stitch. Do not catch cording. Do the same at other end, having one cord on each side of stitching. Gather fabric and tie at bottom. Attach desired embellishment to safety pin, to make removable. Repeat Steps 2 and 3 for each corner. Pin embellishments to bottom of gathers. Remove gathers to store tablecloth flat.

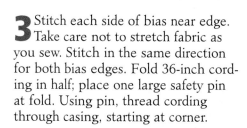

POINSETTIA GOBLET COASTER

Spark up your holiday events and your glassware with a few colorful and elegant poinsettia coasters.

MATERIALS

- Paper and pencil for pattern
- Fabric, tightly woven with some sheen
- Fusible web
- Matching thread
- Metallic thread

TOOLS

- Shears
- Iron
- Sewing machine
- Marking pen
- Water-repellant spray

$

1 On paper, sketch a petal 2½ by 1½ inches. Cut out petal pattern. On larger paper, create poinsettia pattern. Trace five petals, equidistant and forming a circle. Between petals, trace outside part of petal so it looks like it is behind the first group of petals. (Do not worry about each petal being perfectly spaced or shaped.) Cut two 7-by 7-inch pieces of fabric and one 7-by 7-inch piece of fusible web. Place web between fabric, wrong sides together. Press to fuse.

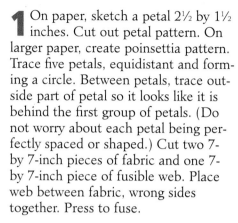

2 Center poinsettia pattern on fabric; trace around outside of pattern. Use petal pattern to trace the rest of the petal at every other petal. Using matching thread (photo illustrates stitching lines with contrasting thread) and narrow, fairly short zigzag stitch, follow marking for full petals. Leave an unstitched space in center, then stitch around secondary petals. Pull threads to back and tie knots.

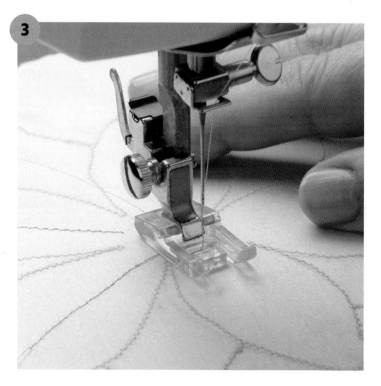

3 Using metallic thread, stitch petal veins starting with long center one. Stitch veins going out from stitching line. Secure thread to back as in Step 2. If your machine makes dots, or a similar shape, stitch 3 to 5 in center. Just outside stitching line, cut around edges. Press. Apply water-repellant spray to help prevent stains.

INDEX